A Heart Torn, A Soul Mended:

A Bereaved Parent's
Search for Harmony

Tricia Wolfe
Foreword by Alan Pedersen

Ferne Press

Summary: A woman's life experiences come full circle after the death of her son.

Library of Congress Cataloging-in-Publication Data
Wolfe, Tricia
A Heart Torn, A Soul Mended: A Bereaved Parent's Search for Harmony
/Tricia Wolfe–First Edition
ISBN-13: 978-1-933916-79-8
  1. Memoir 2. Bereavement 3. Survivor
I. Wolfe, Tricia II. Title
Library of Congress Control Number: 2010938982

The views expressed by the author are hers alone and are not representative of the views of the publisher.

Manufactured by Friesens Corporation
in Altona, Manitoba, February 2011
Docket 63722

FERNE PRESS

Ferne Press is an imprint of Nelson Publishing & Marketing
366 Welch Road, Northville, MI 48167
www.nelsonpublishingandmarketing.com
(248) 735-0418

For my son Brad who births
a new life in me every day

Foreword

BY ALAN PEDERSEN

At a Bereaved Parents Conference in St. Louis, Missouri, I had the great fortune to meet Tricia Wolfe. We were both presenters at the conference and quickly struck up a conversation about our loss and work. After hearing the story of the tragic death of her son Brad, I was amazed at her determination to use her pain and journey as a light of hope for others. Tricia's passions for touching lives became evident to me as I listened to her describe how she developed her "The Healing Power of Dreams" presentation.

We became instant friends, and I became a fan of her insight into the vital role the subconscious mind plays in helping us connect with our pain and heal after experiencing tragedy and loss. Patricia's background as a caregiver, mixed with her own real-life experience as a bereaved mother, led her to writing this wonderful book.

Over the years, I have had the honor of meeting thousands of bereaved families as I speak and play music for organizations that help those going through grief. There is no doubt in my mind that this book will help those who are hurting from life's deepest losses.

I am honored to recommend Tricia's powerful and inspirational book. May you find your own measure of healing as you share in the story, journey, and healing told intimately from the heart of one who has had her heart so completely broken and yet has found her way to a place of peace.

Alan Pedersen

CHAPTER ONE
Goddess Evolving

I feel like a goddess NOW.

It's very strange, not the way it's supposed to be. I am a woman with grief; the mother of a son too soon deceased. I am a shunned daughter, my family is angry with me. I have few friends, I isolate and avoid people from my past. I dread Christmas especially, but feel trepidation as other annual celebrations approach.

And yet, I have been awakened. Released. Freed from so much of the pain I carried, liberated from the bondage of the past. My son is my catalyst. His death dissolved many of the burdens I carried in this life. His death released the creative spirit in me.

I celebrate my body every day now. As I reflect upon my nudity in the mirror, I raise my arms above my head, stretch the feminine me, and smile. I embrace my womanhood. I enjoy my breasts, especially my nipples. These days, I understand. I claim the feminine me that has emerged. Even as I write these words, I feel a pulse in the hollow of my womb.

If we go deep enough into our grief, we have the potential to emerge as "celebratory survivors."

I'm sixty years old as I search for the wisdom of what has happened. In my quest to find the life of my son, to solve the mystery of his sudden death, I have found me. Brad's death sent me spiraling; his violent departure catapulted me into this new realm. My son, who still lives in my heart, gives me the keys. He guides me to the doors I open to an enlightened life. My son's death freed me to become the woman that I am. He celebrates my journey, and he smiles as I discover new passions. Instead of avoiding and withdrawing, I am able to approach social situations with a spirit of discovery.

I sometimes reflect backward. We all do. I've just become more aware of my reflections since my son died. For a time, ruminations of past events consume the thought energies of every bereaved parent. These ruminations are normal and necessary. Regrets and mistakes are often the focal point of these thoughts. This, too, is normal.

Life is a reflection of whys.

There are many life events I didn't plan for, but to regret is to presume you are in control of universal forces. I didn't plan for an out-of-wedlock pregnancy. To regret my pregnancy would be to say my oldest son, Sam, was a mistake. All of my sons are blessings to me. I was raised in a strict Catholic home, so I didn't plan to marry a Lutheran. I have considered how my life would be different if I'd married a Catholic. And I didn't plan on Brad's death when he was only twenty-nine. But these things happened. For me, life is a reflection of *whys*.

Do some of my life's events plague me? Do they weigh constantly on my mind? Yes, they have at times. These thoughts weave their way into my quest for the answer to "Why?"

Released now, I cannot go backward. Healing emerged as I was freed from the bondage of my past. I can no longer subscribe to a society, a church, or even family members who remain in bondage to an archaic system. Masculine energies are held in higher esteem than feminine energies in our society because a patriarchal culture is our heritage. Power, ambition, responsibility, knowledge, and drive are traits our culture uses to measure success. But, how do we measure successful compassion? It is our feminine energies that teach us to nurture, to mother, and to honor relationships.

Be kind to yourself. Be patient.

Bereaved parents are taught this early in grief support groups. Aren't these words familiar? We learn them as Christians from the Bible.

Love is patient, love is kind. It does not envy, it does not boast, it is not proud. It is not rude, it is not self-seeking, it is not easily angered, it keeps no record of wrongs. Love does not delight in evil, but rejoices in the truth. It always protects, trusts, hopes and perseveres (Corinthians 13:4–8).

These words are used during many wedding ceremonies, but don't they have universal application outside conjugal love? I once had a pediatric therapy practice, Child Life Therapy. The therapists who worked for me were dedicated professionals who wanted to improve the lives of their handicapped patients, just as those parents hoped their children's lives would be enhanced.

When the therapists were sick, or wondered about taking time off, or needed a break, I'd often tell them, "You can't help others unless you take care of yourself first. You can't give of yourself if you neglect your own needs."

Through my son's death, I learned to listen to the teachings of my heart and soul.

How little I knew then. I thought these words meant to take good care of yourself in the physical realm. I had no idea how much more important it was to take care of yourself emotionally. Our souls contain a spiritual energy every bit as important as our physical natures. Our hearts hold our life's blood, our emotional energy. When our emotional and spiritual selves are shattered, love is essential to mending those broken pieces.

From within me, I learned to love myself, to mother myself, and to nurture my emotional energy. From without, I had always held physical exercise and energies in high esteem. I liked to look good and eat healthy foods. I also held motherhood in high esteem, that is to say, mothering everyone else. As I emerged from the fog of grief, from the depths of despair, as I tenuously stepped into a world of chaos and picked up the shreds of a bereaved mom's life, I discovered how to mother myself, how to be compassionate to me. To listen to the teachings of my heart. To not do things because I was expected to do them or because another decided what was right for me.

Within the best of my ability, I had always mothered those around me. That was my job. And I took pride and delight in this job. I cooked for others, entertained, did good works, sewed, and reaped the benefits of a nicely furnished home. All of that. I learned how to care for a family from my mother, and I thought if I nurtured others, I would be happy. But as I emerged from grief, I realized that both my mother and father took care of my physical needs, but they didn't know how to nurture my heart. Their inability to give me the unconditional love I needed has wounded them as much as it has wounded me.

I believe we too often emulate the *Martha Stewart model*. Martha shows us how to be a successful woman using masculine energy. She embodies the essence of conventional female success as defined by patriarchs: a decorated and organized home with lovely gardens and delicious foods. The home is the woman's domain, and no one shows us how to beautify our domain better than Martha. She has succeeded and has become wealthy, renowned, and respected for her skills. She enchants us, as she applies her masculine energy to all things domestic. We appreciate Martha for what she gives us. She is our female father.

I believe Oprah Winfrey is popular because she offers us a world of balance between masculine and feminine energies. Daily, she infuses audiences and guests with thoughtful considerations and frivolous delights. She listens to people with compassion, not with judgment. I don't look to Martha as my role model for homemaker status. I want to be more like Oprah. I strive to be honest and kind and have fun with myself.

When I raised my first two children, Sam and Brad, I strived to be both Martha and Mary as Luke describes these women in the Bible.

Jesus came to Bethany, a village about two miles from Jerusalem where Martha opened her home to him. She had a sister Mary, who sat at the Lord's feet listening to what he said. But Martha was distracted by all the preparations that had to be made. She came to Jesus and asked, "Lord, don't you care that my sister has left me to do all the work by myself? I could use a little help around here."

"Martha, Martha," the Lord answered, "you are worried and upset about many things, but only one thing is needed. Mary has chosen what is better and it will not be taken away from her" (Luke 10:39–42, NIV).

Jesus could have spoken these words to me. In my past, I erred on the side of being like Martha. I was out of balance, striving to be the perfect woman as defined by masculine energies. If I could change anything, I'd have spent more time being present, like Mary. Jesus was right; moments shared together last forever.

Life is a process of growth.

During this time period, I've grown so much. But I know there is more to learn as I continue on my journey. Life is a process of growth. I know there's more to come, and I look forward to each step along my expedition.

As senseless as it seems, what happened to my son freed my heart and soul to become who I am today.

Chapter Two

Brad's Death

March 23, 2003, started out like other Sundays for our family. Scott, my adopted son, and I attended the 11:00 a.m. Methodist service. After church, my husband Frank, Scott, and I planned to visit with Brad and his fiancée, Ann, at their home in Holly, Michigan.

Holly is a small town that houses the Holly Rehab Center for the mentally ill. Brad went there for treatment when he was diagnosed as bipolar with psychotic tendencies.

When we came home from church, Frank told me about the phone calls with Brad, our eldest son Sam, Ann, and Dr. Tibb, Brad's psychiatrist. Dr. Tibb called and spoke to Brad while I was at church. Brad yelled and swore at the doctor. He told Dr. Tibb he was just in the profession for the money. When Frank spoke with Brad, Brad said he didn't want me to come to Holly because he said I was a food thief.

"Well, that's all the more reason we should go," I said. "If Brad is *that* sick, we need to be there."

As a mother, I felt responsible for my son's illness and wished to be there to heal him. We went to Holly, even though he didn't want to see me. On our way, I called Ann and learned that Brad had been displaying this *weird smile*. I remembered eleven years ago that smile meant that he was hearing voices. I knew from prior experience that those voices were a psychotic symptom. My next phone discussion was with the doctor, who called in an antipsychotic prescription to a Holly pharmacy. We picked up the medication, in hopes of convincing him to take them.

It had been eleven years since we'd been in this predicament. When Brad lived with us, we always managed to talk to him, calm him, and reason with him. Now he was an independent man. We knew we'd have to get a court order to put him in a hospital if he wouldn't cooperate. We'd have to testify that he was a danger to himself or others.

Once, many years ago, he was taken against his will to the psychiatric ward. That experience was so horrible for all of us that Brad could be convinced to comply with us when he was unstable.

This time, Brad seemed past the point of reason. Frank knew better than to stir up Brad's mania by telling him he needed to go to the hospital. We knew we needed a court order as a threat to get him to cooperate, but it was Sunday. The courts would not be open until the next morning. When we stopped at the police station to alert them that our son was unstable, the dispatcher abruptly said they couldn't help us until we had the order. By the time we arrived at his apartment, Brad wasn't home. With nothing left to do, we returned home, paralyzed.

When Brad wasn't home by late that night, Ann went looking for him. Main Street was blocked with yellow tape, and a police officer stopped and asked her what she wanted. She told him she was looking for her boyfriend, Brad. They instructed her to go to the police station. When she arrived, Ann asked if someone could help her find her boyfriend. After being interrogated about Brad's overall demeanor and alleged disruptive behavior, she was told he was dead.

Ann had a policeman dial our number to deliver the news. Frank answered. Ann told him Brad was dead, that she was at the police station, and they'd taken Brad to the hospital. I rationalized, "*Well, if they took him to the hospital, then he's still alive.*"

I called the hospital and spoke to the emergency room nurse.

When the nurse told me that we should both come, I knew my son was dead. I screamed and prayed and helplessly hoped it wasn't true. I knew it was true, but my mind split off. I bargained. *No, this can't be. Not Brad, not my beautiful son. Oh God, please let him live. There's still time for a miracle. I'll do anything.*

We were like robots as we blanketed Scott, put him in the car, and made our second trip that day to see Brad. Side by side, we felt the absence of pain as the absence of life.

I bargained, "There's still time for a miracle."

We knew the director of the Holly Rehab Center. He met us in the ER waiting room and said, "I saw the body. It's Brad."

He brought two staff women with him. One of them stayed with Scott while a social worker shuffled Frank and me back into the emergency area. He explained, "A policeman is standing guard in the room with your son's body. You'll have to view the body from the hallway."

"You mean I can't even say goodbye to my son in private? I'm his mother, and I can't even go in the room and hold his hand?" I pleaded, desperate to get in the room where he lay, to touch him one last time.

My child is not a body.

"No, that won't be possible. The body is state's evidence."

My child is not a body. Why are they calling my son a body? This is not right. This is wrong.

I screamed. I wrapped my arms around my chest, bent over, and howled. I felt the social worker's panic when he asked me, "Are you going to be all right?"

I knew I had to calm down, or I'd never get to see my son. I controlled myself and was escorted back to the waiting room where Scott watched TV. I sat next to the other staff person from Holly Center. She was a stranger to me, but I sensed that the director had brought her to help us on that horrible night. We sat still, the uncomfortable nearness of two strangers physically close together in a tragic moment.

"Are you Brad's sister?" she asked.

I smiled through my tears. I looked a wreck. Black eye makeup

I knew those words were his parting gift to me.

mixed with salty tears clouded the circles under my swollen eyes. My cheeks felt wet and naked from the strain.

"No. I'm Brad's mother."

In the silence then I knew Brad's spirit had just passed through. I knew those words were his parting gift to me. That he wanted to touch me with his love and tell me he could see the beauty within. I knew he was a kind and sensitive person, that he wanted me to smile in spite of my pain. I believe he wanted me to always remember that strange woman's words to me in the emergency room of his death.

We never were permitted to be with Brad in private. The county sheriff's department and the hospital attorney dismissed our pleadings. Since my son was "state's evidence," access to the room where he lay was denied. These were routine legal procedures for the suspicious circumstances of his death. We said our goodbyes through a screened window where Brad's bloody nakedness rested on a metal table, covered with a white sheet. I saw blood and cuts all over his shoulders and face. I saw bruises and the breathing mask and tube that hung from his slack mouth. I thought about him being naked, and I knew there were more cuts and bruises under that sheet. When I saw him, I saw my child, not the twenty-nine-year-old man he'd become. And I thought, *How could my sensitive, kind, helpful, sweet-natured son who had been through so much and worked so hard to achieve and accomplish so many of his goals—goals he modified so often because of his mental illness and the hand injury from when he was younger—and who had traveled through so much pain and climbed so many moun-*

tains in such a short time have his life ended so abruptly and cruelly?

I cried, "I love you," and I sobbed goodbye.

Brad crossed over the evening of March 23, 2003. I don't think I'll ever find out exactly what happened. Some have spoken to the guys who were there that night, but they don't want to talk about it. When the cops told everyone to leave the apartment and that they would take care of Brad, everyone left. Everyone except Dante. It was his apartment, and he'd made the 911 call.

I was not there, and I've had to piece together what occurred that night. This is what I believe happened to my son on that Sunday evening.

Brad went to Joe's apartment in the early evening to retrieve his power screwdriver, which Joe had borrowed. Brad found Joe hanging out next door, at Dante's apartment. Brad sat in a chair next to the fish tank and began to poke at the fish with a pencil. Dante told him to quit. Brad became agitated and threw something. Brad was strong and his throw damaged the wall. Then Brad stood up, said he was going to leave if he wasn't welcome, and he tripped. As he fell forward, he crashed onto a glass coffee table.

I believe a woman cop came and threatened Brad, trying to get him to go with her. Brad refused. Although Brad was normally compliant, his mania would have enabled him to defy authority. She pulled her gun on him and called for back-up. Still, Brad refused to cooperate. A male cop arrived and snuck behind Brad while the other cop taunted and pointed her gun at him. The male cop pulled Brad's arms from behind, threw him to the ground, and knelt on top of him. Brad cried out, "I can't breathe," but they were busy putting on the cuffs. The cops called an ambulance once they realized he wasn't breathing.

Brad had no gun, no knife, and no drugs. The newspapers reported that the cops went to a hospital to be checked for injuries that night, and I believe that they were covering themselves. The only blood on their hands was Brad's.

Three months after Brad's death, I was told the county coroner determined cause of death was "Positional Compression Asphyxiation." The funeral director called to tell me this news, since he was the one who had received the official document issued by the Oakland County coroner's department. When I found out the cause of death was asphyxiation, my first thought was: *Maybe his death came quieter than I thought; maybe I won't be so tormented with those violent visions at night.*

I'd known my son's death was bloody. At night and during the day, I was plagued by the visions of lacerations on his body that I'd seen through the window of the hospital room. I was tortured by the sight of his head contusion as prominent as a tennis ball on the front of his skull when I first saw his body laid out at the Holly funeral home. I recalled how we asked Ann to run back to the house to find Brad's cap so we could cover that bulge. For three months after his death, I assumed the cause of death was a head injury. As I sorted through this new information, I felt the same emotions I felt when Ann called to tell us Brad died.

The cops should have known better, but they were poorly trained.

The cops should have known better, but they were poorly trained. Frank had been a volunteer with Alliance for the Mentally Ill (A.M.I.) members who offered police training on managing people with mental illness. A.M.I. presented workshops to different precincts and taught police officers how to work with people with various mental disorders such as bipolar, schizophrenia, autism, and Alzheimer's disease.

But the Oakland County police departments always refused A.M.I.'s help. They said they knew how to handle difficult situations. Yes, cops do receive training in their academies. That evening, their actions toward my son were punitive and threatening, consistent with their training and mind-set.

On the Saturday night before he died, Brad told Ann about the dream he'd had the night before.

"I dreamed about Paco—that I was flying above in the skies with him."

Although Frank and I missed the signs of our son's impending death, Brad received a sign. He dreamed that he would soon be in flight with his deceased bird.

GENTLE POINTS

- Mental illness is a disease. Like diabetes, it is a disease that requires vigilant attention in order to acquire chemical balance.

- Unlike diabetics, the mentally ill may not be capable of monitoring their chemical and emotional stability. Sugar and insulin levels and physical symptoms are easier to measure than psychotropic medication levels and behaviors.

- Fortunately, we live in an age where there are hundreds of psychotropic medications available to facilitate chemical balance in the mentally ill brain.

- Psychotropic meds are not the same as a daily insulin injection. Chemical balance in the mentally ill person's brain depends on regular, reliable, and supportive individuals who seek to understand the link between behavior and medications. It is not as simple as taking or not taking a pill.

- The stigma of mental illness needs to dissolve. The more we talk openly and share our experiences of loved ones, the more we will learn and better be able to treat this illness.

CHAPTER THREE

Funeral

The vision of my son's last moments cycled through my brain all night long. I lamented over and over how I couldn't even kiss him goodbye, hold his hand, or hug him. I begged for mercy from the scenes I created of his last traumatic moments when he was victimized.

Some label the initial stages of grief as the numb stage, as if there is no feeling. I wish. When I think of numb, I think of anesthesia, of unconsciousness, of going to a place where I have no memory of what happened. That's not how I felt at all.

Bereaved parents are not unconscious or without memory. I was awake and alive to the procedures which claimed my son's life. I felt the pain of his life being ripped from me. It is a pain beyond any parent's imagination. In order to withstand the trauma, my spirit medicated the wounds of my severed heart so my body and mind could function through a fog, not in numbness. With that foggy awareness, I proceeded with the machinations of coffin selection, phone calls, funeral arrangements, and a grave site decision. Let there be no mistake—with my heart I saw, and felt, and can remember every torturous step.

Monday we met with two funeral directors and notified three pastors that we needed their services. We arranged two funerals and

Bereaved parents are not unconscious or without memory.

two viewings—one in our hometown and one in Holly. We wanted Brad's friends and colleagues who'd known him those years he lived in Holly to have the opportunity to say goodbye.

On Tuesday, we had the Holly viewing. The place was packed. Dr. Tibb told us that Brad was now free from the pain of his illness. The parlor was stuffed with the mentally ill, caregivers of the mentally ill, and Brad's friends and work colleagues. All of Frank's coworkers were there and all of Ann's family came. I felt a bitter sweetness as so many people from so many walks of life came to give their condolences.

The two funeral services were each customized for my son's unique spirituality. Brad deserved an interdenominational final farewell. Our son now rested with the Communion of Catholic Saints, and I knew that he was with Christ.

Twice, I needed to get up in the morning and get dressed to prepare for my child's funeral. Funeral gatherings are necessary rituals. I wonder, is the ritual designed to support a bereaved parent during their grief or to give others an opportunity to do their duty?

On Friday, after the burial, our families came back to our home. During that family time together, I got mad at Frank's sister for talking about stupid stuff. She told me I could preserve the funeral flowers by hanging them upside down and doing this or doing that, just like she had done at her daughter's wedding. This was a time to mourn, not celebrate.

I was mad at my brothers and their wives. I was mad at their children, my nieces, for saying nothing and for leaving so early, with leftovers that I packed for them, like we'd just had a party at Pat's house in Michigan. I was mad at Aunt Ellen for being so selfish, so intent on making sure she had some baked goods to take home.

And I was mad I had to pack sandwiches for everyone, like this was some sort of holiday. I was especially mad at Jane's son, Scott's birth uncle, for his arrogance, for being him, acting like he was entitled to have mayonnaise on his sandwich, and of course I would look through the kitchen and do whatever it took to make his sandwich pleasing to him. That it wasn't good enough to have the mustard and ketchup that were already out. Why couldn't his mother look for the mayonnaise? Why did I have to make this boy's sandwich? None of this made sense to me.

So much shared ritual. By Saturday morning, I had to be alone. When Frank's family came over to say goodbye, I refused to see them. I covered my head with a towel and spent the rest of the day in my bedroom. Had to grieve alone. In darkness. I covered the windows. Sunlight hurt. It hurt to move. I sat still for hours. If I moved, if I opened my eyes, I felt pain. Everyone and everything either hurt me or made me angry.

I was mad at God, too. I told him to go pick on someone else. I told him my name wasn't *Job*. Pastor Bill, the Assemblies pastor, said, "It's okay to be mad at God. He's a big guy."

It's okay to be mad at God. He's a big guy.

A month later, I returned to the Methodist church to participate in their Homeless Week, a period of seven days when that church opens its doors to the homeless from Detroit and provides food, shelter, entertainment, and prayer. Since I was chairman of that ministry, I believed my attendance was necessary. I was present in body, but my mind was only on my son. That was the week I realized Brad would never have any children, that I would never know any grandchildren from him. Then I really got angry at God and dared him to perform a miracle and let Ann be pregnant. But she wasn't, and so I went around just saying "shit" and "fuck" and "this whole thing sucks" and that's the best way to describe my feelings.

I didn't want to leave the house. I called people only if I absolutely had to. I retired from everything—Junior Great Books, Bible Study Fellowship, Cub Scouts, helping in the classroom, church, Church and Society ministry, working out, working in. I didn't want to do anything, go anywhere, and most of all, I did not want to see or talk to anyone. Every time I saw someone or had to talk to someone, all

I could do was cry. More calls, more tears, more isolation. The only place I wanted to be was at the grave site. I could sob there. No one needed to be embarrassed by tears. Over time, the amount of sobbing there grew briefer. I could smile at times, after I read the inscriptions on the markers of the graves that surrounded Brad's. I noted with bittersweet pleasure that two young female bodies were near his.

When a child dies, the parent's life is like shattered glass.

In those first months of my grief, I felt like I was drowning. Surrounded by a sea of torment, I felt lost. All I could do was tread the water and hope I'd find some land to grab onto someday. I was exhausted. Eventually, I washed up on a shore. There, all I could do was crawl and clutch at the ground I was washed upon. But the ground was so barren. I felt like I was on an island in the middle of nowhere, alone and helpless.

Real life was a mass of sympathy cards, thank you notes, crying, and anger. Some days, I tried sleeping without the sleep medication Dr. Tibb had prescribed for me. Those nights, I tossed and turned and visualized how horrible my son's last minutes must have been. When I got out of bed, I knew I'd have a bad day, a day that grew worse as I slid backward into despair. Those days I couldn't do anything except cry. I'd stop sobbing one minute, get up, do laundry, then have to sit down and cry, get up, put away dishes, and then sit and cry. If anyone called on a day I hadn't slept, I'd tell them I couldn't think or do anything except feel my sadness. A sleeping pill became essential for my survival.

Holidays are the bane for a bereaved parent. With Easter coming in the next month, I realized that my family was less supportive about my son's death than they could have

Like shattered glass, the pieces of a bereaved parent's life are fragile.

been. My family seemed insensitive to my grief. To this day, Frank's family has never called me since Brad died. My mother-in-law never wrote or called me or sent me a card. Neither she nor my mother ever offered any assistance in writing thank you notes, nor did they ever suggest that someone from the family could help me. And I didn't know any better. No one offered to help with anything, and I didn't think to ask. I'd never read anything about how a grieving mother is supposed to act. I didn't know I needed someone from my family or a friend—anyone, really—to help me write thank you notes. Besides, I wasn't grateful. It's not the same as when a parent or an elderly loved one dies and the nice flowers and plant arrangements become a cherished memory of a full life, now passed. When a child dies before the parent, life is out of order. Both the bereaved parent and the nonbereaved are confronted with the unthinkable.

It was not a loving, kind, or supportive family member who showed me the road toward healing grief. Over time, through ignorance, gentleness, and trauma, I stumbled onto roads that revealed the unconditional love of a divine universe.

GENTLE POINTS

- When a child dies, the parent experiences a severed heart. It is an amputation that lasts forever.

- Both an amputee and a bereaved parent cannot reach back in time and reattach their leg or their child to their physical life.

- An amputee can learn to walk again, but he is never the same. He will always be an amputee. So, too, is a bereaved parent always a bereaved parent.

- The bereaved parent travels a new journey in life, one that never forgets the pain of their loss. It is a journey that includes an awareness of their child's life.

- Healing comes to the bereaved parent as they embrace their wound and affirm their pain.

- When we discover universal truths, we are able to walk on a journey that heals.

CHAPTER FOUR

Walking Through Grief

I n America, people have an attitude of stoicism. We are not a culture that condones displays of emotions, especially sadness. And my family was no exception. Brad's death was traumatic enough, but my family was incapable of comforting me.

I needed support, a good listener. I needed to share my grief.

In the months and years when Brad's death was so fresh, I felt ignored, criticized, and scolded for my actions and my inactions. I became the guilty victim, the wounded one who was blamed for others' inability to accept the victimized me. My family did not

We are not a culture that condones displays of emotions, especially sadness.

know what to do. They had no concept of just being present for me. They wanted to fix me. They didn't know how to listen to a bereaved mother cry out her anguish. Each time they judged, dismissed, or blamed me for not getting better, the wounds of my grief deepened.

A traumatic incident with my spouse led me to Sister Lucia, a counselor. She serviced me through First Step, the county's counseling center for abused women. I wasn't sure I fit there, since I wasn't physically abused. But I learned that I had been emotionally abused.

Lucia opened the eyes of my soul when she validated the trauma I'd experienced from my son's death. I learned that my own existence, as well as my son's, was denied when my requests for help and my expressions of pain were ignored. Although she was a nun, Lucia did not preach to me. She showed me how women are typically regarded by Christian spouses and by Catholic mothers and fathers. Once a week for nearly a year I sobbed in Lucia's office. The tears that flowed were bitter waters that needed to emerge from my soul. The grief I carried from my son's death overflowed there. Lucia's words then became an essential salve. She often told me I was a good person. I don't know what she saw, but I clung to those words. No one had ever validated me in that way before. She soothed the rawness of my soul as we probed through my grief.

Lucia told me, "Brad's sudden and violent death traumatized you. Yours is not an ordinary grief; it is complicated due to the circumstances surrounding his death. You are a very caring and sensitive woman. The heart cannot carry that much pain forever. You will seek a way to lessen the pain from within yourself."

Lucia suggested that my grief symptoms were akin to post-traumatic stress disorder and the lack of support I experienced pushed me further into myself, but eventually I would find a way out. She was right. The way out of the pain of Brad's death has been an awakening to the feminine me, the totality of my being.

The heart cannot carry that much pain forever. You will seek a way to lessen the pain from within yourself.

I learned that my suffering was real and that I should not rely on others. In *Trauma and Recovery: The Aftermath of Violence—from Domestic Abuse to Political Terror* by Judith Herman, I read how people sympathize more readily when someone has been traumatized by "acts of God," like fires or hurricanes, or even by a disease like cancer. These phenomena give people a chance to rally around, link to a cause, and feel good about fundraiser actions. But when a traumatic event is caused by humanity, such as domestic abuse, rape, or a violent act toward another human being, people struggle to understand how this could happen. They wonder, *What did the victim do to bring this on themselves?*

Nothing about Brad's death or my sorrow was comfortable for my family or friends. I felt abandoned by family in my grief. I wanted so badly for everyone to talk about everything. Bad things had happened to me, but no one would talk to me about it. No one chose to rally around a mom whose son was killed by cops.

I could speak of my sorrow during meetings with other bereaved parents and in Lucia's office. There I was allowed to remember and mourn. There the door opened for my transformation. The truth of my horrors needed to be expressed and validated. Only in safe surroundings could I open my soul to the reality of my sadness. As the truth of my trauma and my sadness was acknowledged, healing waters trickled in and soothed the raw spaces of my emptied soul.

I learned that I was on a solo journey, looking for inner peace. In my loneliness, I could affirm me. Anyone who has experienced severe trauma needs to find a safe outlet where the reality of that trauma can have full expression.

Anyone who has experienced severe trauma needs to find a safe outlet where the reality of that trauma can have full expression.

As my counseling sessions progressed, Lucia queried me about childhood memories. She graphed the relationships between and among my birth family members. I was stunned with what I saw. Tons of relationship energy flowed between my parents and my brothers. Granted, much of it was negative as my mom always worried about my brothers getting into trouble. Lucia suggested that I'd learned to keep a lid on my gregarious nature so I would not cause my parents any anxieties. She also hinted that perhaps my mother was jealous of her daughter.

During one session I recalled many of the comments made on that day I'd last visited in Cleveland for the birthday party my mother had organized for herself. I remembered no one spoke of Brad except my mom, who mentioned him before we went to the restaurant.

"Dad and I just finished doing our will. We hadn't included Scott before, so it worked out pretty well. We substituted Scott's name in our inheritance for Brad."

I was devastated.

When we returned to my parents' home for cake, I tried to stay invisible. I just wanted to wait out the time until we could travel back to Michigan.

Mom came into the living room where I was and asked, "What's wrong with you?"

I said, "Nothing. I'd just rather be in here where it's quieter."

I didn't realize it at that moment, but I was overwhelmed by so many hurtful things said to me that day. I just wanted to bide my time and leave as soon as possible.

When she returned to the hubbub, my aunt asked, "What's wrong with Pat?"

"Nothing," said my mom. "She's just pouting."

On the following Monday, my mother called and suggested that if I felt so bad, I'd better see a doctor. Maybe my hormones were bad. I told her I'd been to a doctor, and I was in good physical health. The only thing wrong with me was grief.

She handed the phone to my dad and told him, "You talk to her."

My dad asked me, "What's wrong with you? Why did you hurt your mother's feelings at her party?"

I said, "Dad, I'm depressed. The only thing I want to do is dig a hole next to Brad and be buried there."

He hung up the phone. I felt like a little girl who'd been abandoned by her parents in a scary jungle of grief.

I told Lucia how my brother also called that Monday night. The event had been but a year since Brad's death.

"Hi, Pat. I hope you won't take this the wrong way. Sometimes, even as adults, we need to be made aware of how we have hurt others. You may not realize it, but our mother was very hurt by your behavior yesterday. She was almost in tears. How could you ruin her eightieth birthday?" asked my brother.

"What did I do?" I asked.

I can't believe my brother is calling to scold me. No one thought of how upset I was, how I was the one who needed consoling.

I thanked my brother for calling. What could I do? I still wore my old obedient habits and continued to navigate in that patriarchal culture, the only world I'd ever known.

I am now at a place where I feel sadness for my parents. They are encumbered by outdated rules and baggage that impaired their ability to join me in my grief journey. My parents are in bondage to an old system, a righteous, masculine-driven culture that believes in being right, no matter the cost. Having a relationship with their daughter is not as important as being obedient, fixing what is wrong, and judging bad behavior. My parents believe they are entitled to determine the proper code of conduct for their bereaved daughter.

People give themselves permission to act mean. The art of kindness pales when people perceive they've been wronged. I reject meanness and unkind words. I disengage myself from situations that are ego-driven and from people and places that tilt too heavily on the masculine side. I seek a connection with universal truths and unconditional love. I look for paths that foster growth and a connection to my son who lives where there is balance between masculine and feminine energy. My soul survival depends on giving myself permission to embrace the feminine side of the scales. The scales of life have tilted on the masculine side long enough.

The scales of life have tilted on the masculine side long enough.

In one of my last counseling sessions, Lucia told me, "Pat, you'll come out of this grief journey better than before you began."

Those words always upset me when I hear them, no matter who says them. Like I was some kind of nincompoop before Brad died—like I was uncompassionate or less of a person. Classic comments like "You'll be more compassionate" or "You'll be able to help others" make me feel like my past deeds and the compassion I had before weren't good enough, that I required more training in the boot camp of life, and that's why my son died.

But Lucia went on to explain, "Our lives, our inner beings, are like an iceberg, with only the tip showing. When we experience trauma, especially extreme trauma, as you have since your son died, or chronic trauma, as you experience from your family's ongoing jabs, more of the iceberg that is you may be revealed. It's not a matter of a *better you* that will emerge, it is *more of you*. Before his death, much of your iceberg was buried under the waters of the cultural roles you assumed. As you continue through your journey, as the painful waters recede, more and more of you will be revealed. You will have a greater understanding of you, a revelation, and an emergence of the you that had been buried by guilt and by pleasing others."

> *It's not a matter of a better you that will emerge, it is more of you.*

Counseling gave me a glimpse of my own history, my birth family, my marriage, and my Catholicism, and how my past intertwined with my present. Counseling gave me permission to be okay with my feelings and with my choices. For example, knowing that holidays and special occasions are difficult for me, I've decided it's okay not to attend.

I am selective about the graduations, showers, weddings, and funerals that I attend. Especially in the early years of my grief, I needed to protect myself from triggers of pain. Most often family and friends are naïve to those of us who carry bruised and fragile hearts. They choose to remain clueless to the tender hearts of bereaved parents.

"Jason just graduated from business school, and he's had three job offers."

Brad died so soon after he graduated from U. of M. He struggled so to find a job.

"Oh, I haven't seen you in so long. You probably don't know Ginny is pregnant with our first grandchild. We're so excited."

Brad can never have any children, and Sam and his wife don't want any. I've worked so hard at foregoing my longing for grandchildren.

"Your mom and I are so happy with our lives. We are so proud of all our children and grandchildren."

My son is dead. Your grandson. He died nine months ago. Why are you telling me this?

"We're so busy. Between our son who lives in Chicago and our daughter who lives in Ohio, we stay on the road visiting."

My family only comes to visit upon request, when I make all the plans and provide the food. I practically have to beg them to come to Michigan. Frank's family ignores me and Scott. I feel as if we don't even exist for them. They've never come to visit since Brad died and send nothing to their grandchild, not even a birthday card.

"How was your Thanksgiving?"

I hate all holidays.

Thoughtless words are like sparks of fire for bereaved parents. As a newly bereaved mom, I measured the amount of fumes I would encounter. Before Brad's death, I relished social gatherings. Life is supposed to be about sharing good times and joyful memories. Sadly, the non-bereaved tends to disconnect from the sorrow of a bereaved parent.

> *Thoughtless words are like sparks of fire for bereaved parents.*

As far as my family is concerned, our relationship has gone downhill since my mom's eightieth birthday party. Interactions with them became a losing battle for me. I tried to communicate my grief and my needs for comfort. I suggested ways they could reach out, and I offered them opportunities to soothe me. Every time I asked for something or explained my truth, I became the guilty victim. My mother once asked me, "Why do you have to punish the rest of us just because you're sad?"

I can only be who I am—a bereaved mom, a grieving sister, your only daughter who has learned not to yearn for the unconditional love that you are unable to provide.

I would love to have my family understand, accept, and appreciate me for who I am now.

As a child, I was taught you go to heaven if you live a good life. As an adult, all of my Christian religious experiences taught me that heaven is a better place. My faith was built from many foundations. With little comfort and support from my family, would it be my faith heritage that would give my soul the nourishment I needed to survive?

GENTLE POINTS

- "Sorrow makes us children again. It destroys all differences in intellect. The wisest know nothing" (R.W. Emerson).

- Being present is the most precious gift the nonbereaved can give to the bereaved.

- Bereaved parents need to cry and to sob. They need not apologize or be ashamed of their tears.

- Tears are healing waters. They are songs from our soul.

- Emotional displays of sadness are healthy expressions for the bereaved. Our pain is released. Denial and avoidance bury our emotional energy.

- Recovery from trauma is like walking through fires. One's exterior baggage is burned away.

- Grief is real. It is a journey the bereaved must walk through.

- Bereaved parents need to talk about their deceased child's life. To deny talking about their child denies their child's very existence.

CHAPTER FIVE

Religion

I learned early there are two kinds of people in the world: Catholics and non-Catholics. My religious odyssey began in Catholicism. I liked being a Catholic. It was like belonging to an exclusive club. Since at least half of my community belonged to the same club and my entire family belonged to their local Catholic club, I lived and breathed among my own. We all knew the rules and shared the secret rituals. Rituals are what I appreciate most about the Catholic religion. No one does pomp and circumstance better than Roman Catholics, whose traditions were inherited straight from Rome.

I learned a lot about Mass as a child. Mass is a more complex ritual than the typical Protestant Sunday service. Knowing this ritual is crucial to full participation in the private club. Mass is a sacrifice of the Eucharist. The arrangement of prayers and sequence of activities was built around the Old Testament procedures for offering a sacrifice.

The Mass ritual became less secretive when it changed from Latin to English, around 1963. This change to the vernacular came because of Vatican II, around the time I was in high school.

> *Rituals are what I appreciate most about the Catholic religion.*

Catholics attend Mass on Sundays because they are obligated. I was raised to believe that our soul is marked with mortal sin if we do not attend. Catholics celebrate Christ's death when they go to church on Sunday. They are not there to sing praise but to join the priest as he offers up the Eucharist to Father God in order to atone for our sins, starting with Eve's original sin.

There are seven sacraments in the Catholic Church, one being Holy Communion. Before receiving the sacrament of Holy Communion, as second graders we were taught about sins, confession, and the proper procedures for receiving the sacrament of Penance. Penance is necessary to cleanse one's soul so as to be worthy enough to receive Communion.

Sins blacken the soul, and the only way to become pure is through confession. If a Catholic dies with unconfessed sins on their soul, they need to spend some time in Purgatory, a sort of holding tank that burns off sins. If your sins are small, like lying and disobedience, they're venial sins. If they're huge, like murder, they're mortal. Unless that sin is confessed, the sinner goes directly to hell when he/she dies.

I received my religious and elementary school education, grades one through eight, from one of the local Catholic parish schools in Ohio. Our confessions were in a confessional, a darkened cubicle where the priest sat in the middle and we confessors knelt on a pew on either side of the priest. The priest slid open a window to signal the confessor's turn to tell how many, how often, and which sins blackened your soul the past week. Adults and children lined up on Saturday afternoons for the chance to purge themselves of their sins.

After I'd confessed my venial sins, the priest assigned me a few Hail Marys and Our Fathers as my penance. I always said my penance immediately. I liked to leave the confessional cubicle, kneel at the pews, and say my prayers fast. I felt it was a stigma, a reflection of how black my soul was, if I knelt there very long.

My husband was raised in the Lutheran church. Frank was a good and moral man but an agnostic at best, perhaps an atheist. I didn't know this when we dated. I thought Frank was a spiritual person, a devout Lutheran. He brought me Daily Devotionals each month. I was impressed. I'd never read such real prayers, stories of life told from the heart with Bible verses included. My prayer training was rote and memorized. I read these devotionals from his church every day, and I believed he too was reading them. I fantasized how we would always share this wonderful world of spirituality. Catholic doctrine was not as important to me as where a person's heart lay. Much later, I realized his mother sent him those books. Frank was more than happy to give them to me. He wasn't reading them, except when we read them together.

A difference between Lutherans and Catholics is the way these two institutions view Mary, Christ's mother, the blessed virgin. As taught to me, this idea of a virgin mother totally confused my sexuality, my female essence. This teaching is a lie. Birth mothers can't be virgins. As Catholic girls and boys, we learned to honor and worship Mary for her obedience and submissiveness. The traditional Virgin Mary builds an absurd image of an ideal, chaste female.

As taught to me, this idea of a virgin mother totally confused my sexuality, my female essence.

What I learned about Mary played out in my and Frank's relationship. I was the yielding virgin whom my partner expected would always be the sweet and accommodating wife.

The role of a woman in Frank's Lutheran family is to serve the male ego. Be a good homemaker and mother and be available for procreation. It is my belief that women are not adored; they're taken for granted.

My feminine essence was birthed in the Catholic faith and bred in the Lutheran faith. No wonder I was confused about my femininity.

Though I had my children baptized in the Catholic Church, I struggled to find a religious community. I was looking for a nurturing community and spiritual inspiration. At the same time, I was plagued by my Catholic roots, which dictated that my children must receive the sacraments. For a time then, I made everyone attend Mass on Sundays. As difficult as it was for me to step away from the Catholic rituals I cherished, it was equally difficult to step back into them, especially since I was the lone spiritual ranger in the family.

Over the years, we attended several churches and even held family worship in our home. Still, something was missing. During those years, I now know that my own soul, my spiritual energy, was not being touched by those patriarchal religions. Mentally, though, I was comfortable. I'd done my best to provide my sons' souls a connection to their spirituality.

After Brad was diagnosed with bipolar disorder and became suicidal, I found a church that embraced me and nourished me: my local Assembly of God church. I stumbled into this church one day after Brad had threatened to commit suicide.

"God, I am so broken. I love my son so much. He is so precious. His pain is killing me. I don't know what to do. I don't know how to help him. I don't understand. Why couldn't he have a physical problem, something I have experience in healing? I don't know where to go. I don't know what's wrong. How did this happen? I am nowhere. Nothing matters. Please help me, help my son."

I left the church feeling lighter. I felt God had heard my pleas and knew I needed to return. I picked up a brochure and attended service the following Sunday.

I felt God had heard my pleas.

The aura at the Assemblies Church was like a welcome home party. Everyone was so friendly, seemed so glad that I'd come. I felt embraced by the community from the moment I entered. Once inside, I could hardly believe my ears. Everyone was singing. There was shouting of "Amen" and "Praise God" and people stood and waved their hands. Some moved their bodies with their eyes closed to the music. The words were prominently displayed on a big screen, so I didn't have to thumb my way through a hymnal to find the song. I was silent that first Sunday, an observer.

From spring 1992 through fall 1999, I joined other souls who travel the born again, charismatic road of Christianity. I enrolled in

Bible studies and went on an evangelical mission trip to Moldova. I was dunked in the big tub that sat up on the platform with the cross and the pulpit. I taught Sunday school. I learned to pray the Assemblies way. I was prayed for. Brad was prayed for. I cried. I was comforted. I believed God had led me to this church and I blessed Him for His guidance. And I prayed. Lots of prayer energy was sent to heaven during those Assemblies years for my son's healing.

I was saved. I opened my heart, and Christ came in. I was no longer an observer but a participant in my own Christian faith. I was filled with the Holy Spirit. I felt like all those tenets of faith I'd been taught as a Catholic were lifted off the pages of the rule book and brought to life. During those years I was an Assembly of God Christian, my heart was aflame with Christian faith, hope, and love. I didn't go to church because I was supposed to. I went because I wanted to, because I felt touched by God's words to me each and every time I went. Just as I embraced the richness of ritual from my Catholic years, so too do I embrace my years of being a charismatic, born again Christian when I felt God's love and not his judgment.

My new religious experience surrounded me with a spirit of love, which guided my struggling soul during the years after my son's death.

My childhood religion built the foundation of the woman I would become.

Gentle Points

- Rituals and remembering help the bereaved soul heal. Examples of helpful gestures:
- Remember the birthday and death date of a bereaved parent's child.
- Show the bereaved that you care by sending a card, calling them on the phone, or visiting them.
- Expect the bereaved to question their faith. Some embrace faith, others reject it, and some discover faith in their journey. No one path works for everyone.

- All prayers are heard. When we pray, we communicate with our Divine Source. Just as our emotional energy needs to be expressed, so too does our spiritual energy need to connect.

CHAPTER SIX
Childhood

I had a normal and blessed childhood. I grew up in a blue-collar community in a suburb of Cleveland.

Normal and enriched. Not rich, not grand, but full. It was filled with family, church, school, and neighborhood playmates. I was born July 30, 1949, to a father who served in the Coast Guard in World War II and a mother who trained as a nurse after high school. My city was a mixture of white European stock, Protestants, and Catholics.

My dad was and still is, even at eighty-six, a handsome man with dark and wavy hair, very little gray, blue eyes, and a square face that softens with dimples when he smiles. I inherited his deep brown hair color and facial architecture. From my mother, I inherited a well-proportioned frame. We both stand at 5'3". We have fine hair, but my mom's is quite thin. She still visits the beauty shop weekly to either have her hair set or fashioned into a hairpiece. I have her brown eyes, and like my mom, I need glasses.

My maternal grandparents came from the poor side of the Ukraine. I relished my Russian heritage, was fascinated by it, and am proud to claim the Ukraine as my ancestry. I craved to learn more about the old country, but my mom's parents didn't care to elaborate because they'd come to America to start over. I always felt loved and valued, comfortable and cozy in their home. Anastasia and George barely stifled the pride in their smile when they posed in pictures with me.

From kindergarten through third grade, I only attended half days of school. My mother often told all of us, "Pat came home from school, ate her lunch and immediately sat at the kitchen table and did her homework. She was such a good student. She never needed any help and never got into any trouble. Not like her brothers."

I guess being no bother was a good thing. I just wish I remembered all this goodness. For the life of me, I cannot recall anything from those early school years, not any teacher or any interaction or action that took place in my life during that time. I don't remember those days when I sat at the kitchen table doing homework.

I do remember I took dance lessons sometime during those years. I wanted to be a ballerina. But I didn't realize that before you prance around on toe shoes, you must practice positioning your feet in ballet slippers. These flimsy slippers and the positioning exercises did not resemble my ballerina image of being on tiptoes. I told my mom I didn't want to take those kind of ballet lessons, that I wanted to dance on my toes. She withdrew me after two lessons.

If I didn't have all of those Holy Communion pictures, I wouldn't know what I looked like back then. One brother arrived when I was four and the other when I was eight. It was almost as if I disappeared, like I didn't exist for a few years. My mom often tells how much work my brothers required. My only childhood memories are of what my mother said: "Pat was such a perfect child. Never caused any problems. She didn't prepare me for the boys. If her brother would have been born first, he'd have been the last."

One of the great things about growing up on my street was easy access to public transportation. I could walk a few blocks to the left of my house and catch a city bus and go wherever my heart desired. Or, I could walk ten blocks to the right and catch an express bus. At either end, the buses connected to the Rapid Transit lines. Thanks to these connections, I became a self-sufficient, independent teenager. When I was fourteen, my first job was at the Cleveland Zoo's concession stand by Monkey Island. At sixteen, I bused myself to Cleveland Psychiatric Institute where I worked for a research doctor and prepared cytology slides. That doctor and that medical experience opened the door to my future career in the medical field.

I experienced the richness of extended family life. Together we celebrated everyone's Baptism, Holy Communion, graduations, wedding showers, and baby showers. On my dad's side, I had seven cousins, so besides the traditional Thanksgiving, Christmas, and Easter get-togethers, we had so many other parties.

My dad's mother, Grandma Johanna, was very special to me. Even today, I wear her mother's ring. Unlike my mom's parents where my brothers and I were the only grandchildren, Johanna had six grand-daughters and four grandsons. While she lived, her grandchildren, like me, had children. When she died, she had at least eighteen great-grandchildren. Yet, I always felt Johanna valued each and every one of us. I know this because she told us. She talked to us. She kept track of all of us. When I visited her home, she always had a display of her grandchildren and great-grandchildren's framed school pictures. She would hold each one, and tell me their name and detailed stories about that child's family. Grandma Johanna was all about family in a quiet, soft way. She'd grown up in an orphanage.

Johanna's four children took turns being hosts for the holidays, and the women shared in the preparation and clean up of all the feasts. We cousins knew each other, we knew our aunts and uncles, and we ate and sang and talked and drank together in each other's homes. It was great. I still miss it.

I experienced the richness of extended family life. I still miss it.

Things were quieter on my mom's side, which was okay with me. It was ethnic and intimate. I spent individualized time with my mom's parents and my aunts Ellen and Joyce. I still am the only girl, grand-daughter, daughter, and niece on my mom's side.

It was in the bosoms of my grandmothers that I experienced unconditional love.

I understand now why memories of my grandparents, especially my two grandmas, came to me first as I write about my childhood and tell how I became me. I did not look to my parents. When I looked there, I saw their physical fondness for me. I was kept clean and neat. I ate three square meals. I learned the rules of proper behavior. Everything in the physical realm that a child needed was provided to me. But it was in the bosoms of my grandmothers that I experienced unconditional love. Two very different women. Two very different styles. But I knew of the love in their hearts for me.

My mother was born organized. Some people are born organized, others learn this skill, and still others never get it. She had a knack for the "one spot" rule, a place for everything and everything in its place. No clutter in our home as everything was neat, folded, and tidy. Over the years, I developed some of my mom's abilities. I had to learn these skills as they did not come naturally to me. I realized the hard way that life was easier and less chaotic if you're organized.

Almost reluctantly, it seemed, my mom let me help with the dusting and vacuuming. My one brother and I washed and dried dishes in those days before dishwashers. I had chores, but I sensed this disinclination on my mom's part to give me domestic responsibilities. I don't know if she thought a child could never meet her standards, or if it was too much bother to make us work, or if she felt it was her job and was threatened by her daughter. I recall she often said, "It's just easier to do it myself."

Since my mom was a nurse, first aid was readily available. My mom is intelligent. I don't remember having any intellectual conversations with her, but one time when we cleaned out the attic, I found her high school report card. She always got all As. My mom read voraciously. At age eighty-five, she still works crossword puzzles and remains articulate and alert.

Mom managed the budget also. Dad often proclaimed how he'd

hand over his paycheck to his wife because she did such a great job of managing the budget.

Dad praised my mom often, held her on a pedestal. She is still held in high esteem by my dad. I not only experienced how smart and organized my mother was, I also heard her talents praised by my dad.

My mom was the Martha Stewart of the fifties, but I am challenged when it comes to knowing where to put things. I once thought to myself when we moved to a new home, *Wouldn't it be great if my mom would come up and help me organize? She's so good at it.*

Upon my request, my mother said, "No, you can do it yourself."

The most disruptive element to our family's rhythm came from my dad's profession. He was an operating engineer—a crane operator—who wore a blue uniform to work. He was around grease and dirt and demolition. A card-carrying member of the International Union of Operating Engineers, he built buildings with the fork of the crane and knocked them down with the boom at the tip of his crane.

Dad didn't have a nine-to-five job. Sometimes he didn't have any job. He was hired by contract. At times, when local jobs were unavailable, he traveled to Dayton and Cincinnati for assignments. A few times when he was out of work and collected unemployment, Mom worked. She did private duty and weekend nursing. Our family's philosophy was that a woman's place was in the home and the man was the breadwinner. My parents struggled during times of financial need. Dad did not want his wife to work outside the home, but at times it became necessary. I don't know how my mom felt about those times when she worked as a nurse. She never discussed the subject with me.

Our family's philosophy was that a woman's place was in the home and the man was the breadwinner.

From pictures, not words, I saw that at one time I was the apple of my dad's eye. As a toddler, I smiled full and wide. I posed so easily with hats fashioned from discarded ladies' pantyhose. Where did that frivolous little girl go?

She reappears in my First Holy Communion pictures. In those photos, I am seven years old, dressed in white, my chin tucked as I smiled demurely and held my rosary and white prayer book. I became a good student, in academics and in church doctrine. I learned to subdue her innate passionate nature.

This combination of subdued passion and handmaiden surrender attracted a Lutheran suitor who pursued me until I became pregnant.

GENTLE POINTS

- Memories, both sad and joyful, are moments to be embraced.

- Our past is now our future. Our past is our history book. We evolve from our history as we move forward into the future. Our book is not baggage to be lugged around with us everywhere we go. Our past need not pull us backward or weigh us down.

- Women hold the womb of creation. Female energy is vital to our universe. It is time to celebrate the passionate energies that are our birthright from our Divine Creator.

CHAPTER SEVEN

Pregnancy Then Marriage

How does a nice Catholic girl who should know better get pregnant? Since I was that nice Catholic girl and it happened to me, I can say it was not the lure of sex. I wasn't thinking about sex all the time, or ever, really. Sure, I wanted a boyfriend, but I wanted someone to hold my hand, put his arm around me, walk with me, and talk with me. I had plenty of girl company. I went to an all-girl high school. I stayed in a girls' dormitory at college, and in the physical therapy program, twenty-two of the twenty-five students were female. I was naïve to the ways of men.

At that time, there was this universal phenomenon about guys. They fantasized about how hot Catholic girls were. Guys assume when girls aren't getting any sex, they are deprived. They assume gals need to orgasm as much as they do. And guys are driven to give us what they perceive we need. This is such a male way of looking at things. If you asked me, I would have said sex was overrated.

I met Frank at a Cleveland State University dance in May 1967 while I was a senior in high school and he was a sophomore at Cleveland State. I don't remember when we first went "all the way," but it didn't take Frank long to seduce me. I was a virgin. Frank was quite matter-of-fact in his expectations of sex. I'm not sure whether he was a virgin at nineteen when we met. I think he was. For us, kissing turned into petting pretty quickly. I tried to resist, but he had a car and money, and he seemed devoted to me. Once, he picked wildflowers from a field and brought them out of the trunk of his car when he saw me. In June 1968, we were engaged.

We choose our mates unconsciously. According to the Imago theory of how couples choose their mates, we choose our mates unconsciously, based on childhood wounds or conflicts that were imprinted in our primitive brain. When we search for a mate, we articulate the thoughts of our new brain. Our new brain houses rational thoughts which makes us believe we have been drawn to a mate who is considerate of us. Perhaps we say we were attracted to our mate because he or she was good-looking and intelligent. These are qualities we are aware of on a conscious level. They are rational thoughts, generated by our cognitive brain.

But our primitive brain, our unconscious, has another agenda. There we have stored the early conditions of our childhood and our childhood wounds. We all have childhood wounds that need to be healed in this life. Thus our unconscious is drawn to a person who resembles our parents' nurturing. We search for a personality we are familiar with, even though that personality frustrated and wounded us.

In my case, Frank has always provided for my physical needs, as my parents did. In my childhood, as in my marriage, I experienced a lack of affirmation, a person who took me for granted, a person who was unable to support me emotionally. My frustrations as a daughter continued as a wife. The Imago theory of coupling makes sense to me. In my marriage, I now see that our cyclical arguments were an engagement of our primitive brain behaviors. Our emotional exchanges were often a replay of unresolved parent-child issues. I realize this as I step back and place distance between these patterns of behavior. It makes sense to my rational brain how I got pregnant without really caring about sex. When I was a hot chick in my twenties, I did what

I'd always done with my parents: I surrendered.

After Frank and I went all the way that first time, I felt committed to our relationship. I believed it was my duty to please my fiancé. Frank always wanted it. I always knew it was coming, so I complied. He was hot and bothered, and I was a willing vessel. Looking back, I now see how subservient I was as a mate.

Before I conceived, our sex was clandestine, which did provide passion and thrill. While the sex act wasn't all that *Sex was an adventure for me.* great, it was always an adventure as to when and where we'd copulate. Besides in the car, we screwed in public park grounds, on my parents' living room couch, in Frank's bedroom in Cleveland, and in his sister's bed in Pennsylvania. Birth control? We used a combination of the rhythm method, rubbers, and pulling out. If I had anything to do over, I'd have gone to a clinic for birth control pills or an IUD. I didn't because my Catholic upbringing taught me that the idea of interfering with God's plan of procreation was abhorrent. Procreation was the main purpose of sex. Have children and populate the world was what I'd learned. The rhythm method was the only sanctioned method of birth control for Catholics. Diaphragms, rubbers, and IUDs put one in a state of sin. How dare a woman interrupt the flow of God's plan with a mechanical device? That's what I was taught by the celibate nuns and priests. Be the obedient wife. Be diligent with my menstrual cycle. I was expected to be responsible for family planning. I was the woman who was expected to know the rhythm of my womb. Another area in which I failed. My periods were rather irregular.

From my perspective, Frank and I broke all the rules when we had premarital sex, so it never occurred to me to further seek a forbidden tool that would prevent the consequences of our unlawful behavior.

So that is how I conceived. Frank's carnal call ruled over my ability to resist: the drive of the flesh reigned over rational thinking. That whole time Frank and I had premarital sex, I felt pulled by my future husband's desires and my need to satisfy him, even though my mind told me, *This is wrong; you're asking for trouble.* It's no small wonder that after we were married, after I delivered the baby, and for the rest of my life when we were free to have sex, I wasn't free. Old baggage clung to my unconscious. So, even though one side of me learned to have orgasms, the other part of me carried shame.

We conceived sometime in November, and I spent the next three months vomiting. I lost fifteen pounds. Whenever Frank and I went somewhere, we had to stop along the way so I could puke on the roadside. Even without being pregnant, I get motion sickness in the back seat of a car, but the sickness of pregnancy surpasses all travel sickness. And there's nothing "morning" about morning sickness. "Morning" just represents the first round of emptying one's stomach contents. For me, it lasted all day, with or without food.

After I completed my junior year at Ohio State University and first year of the therapy program in May 1970, I returned to Cleveland for the summer break. Frank and I rented an apartment and lived together for the first time. We both stayed busy. Being pregnant did not stop me from enrolling in a course at a community college. I knew this would help lighten my academic load when I returned to Ohio State University in the fall with a baby.

Frank graduated that June with his bachelor's degree in mechanical engineering. He worked in the engineering department of a V.A. Hospital.

To be Catholic, pregnant, and unwed was the worst shame ever.

In those days when you were Catholic, pregnant, and unwed, it was considered the worst shame ever. To make matters worse, Frank dismissed me when I tried to explain that I was damaged by being pregnant before marriage.

"You're making a big deal out of it. Where I come from, we don't believe in big weddings anyway."

It wasn't about the wedding. It was about the idea of everyone knowing we were having sex. I was a lost virgin in the eyes of Catholicism. To my family, I was a huge disappointment. When Frank and I announced our elopement and my pregnancy to my parents, my mom said, "You know, Aunt Ellen was planning a big wedding shower for you. We'll have to cancel that. What are we supposed to do with the wedding dress deposit?"

"I'm sorry, Mom."

The wedding dress. That dress was a quick purchase. The summer before the wedding, we went to one store, found a dress on sale that fit, and Mom put some money down. It may have been the second or third one I tried on. I didn't want to make a big fuss for my mom and I didn't want my parents to have to spend a lot of money on a dress for me.

Earlier, I'd asked, "Why can't I wear your dress?"

"It's old-fashioned. You wouldn't like it."

"How do you know? I've never even seen it."

"I'm sure it wouldn't fit."

As shameful as I felt about my pregnancy, once Sam was delivered, I sang "I Feel Pretty" and danced like Natalie Wood did when she performed in *West Side Story*. I sang it silently in the hospital after I nursed, as the nurses took Sam from my arms. And I sang out loud after I nursed him when I was at home. Though I gained thirty pounds during pregnancy, I lost all of it after delivery. I felt beautiful. My female body was transformed. I expanded from a 34B bra with wrinkled cups to an overflowing 34D cup. I came out of both of my pregnancies with bigger boobs, a reduced waistline, and more curvaceous hips. I could have nursed forever.

I loved being a mom. I'd found this cradle inside. I discovered this fountain of nurture that I was unaware existed in me. The mothering instinct. Samuel was my

I loved being a mom.

baby, and I would take care of him. Period. He became my priority, albeit an inconvenient priority. He arrived the summer of my senior year in college, my final year of physical therapy studies. He came in July, the month I was supposed to have a wedding.

Sam was born July 28, weighing eight pounds and nine ounces— a robust, healthy, and happy infant. He was easy to care for, and I enjoyed being his full-time mama those few months before we left

Cleveland for Ohio State University.

Sam's birth spawned in me a passion for all children, as well as compassion for handicapped children and their mothers. I found my niche, my specialty, in pediatric physical therapy. My profession became an intangible gift, a newly discovered talent, an opportunity to be fulfilled while I served others and got paid.

When I returned for the winter term in January, my second term in the physical therapy program, I informed the Ohio State University Physical Therapy School of my name change and my pregnancy. I felt like no physical therapy student in the entire world had ever gotten pregnant while in the program. And no one told me any different. Even though I was married, everyone knew my husband didn't live with me. It was such a small program, so my name change and pregnancy status became known quickly. The therapy program was intense, with lots of labs where we paired off to practice procedures on one another. Pregnancy is a contraindication for many of the procedures, such as diathermy and ultrasound. Therapists must customize the standard prone position when a pregnant woman requires a back massage. All therapy curriculums teach students how to accommodate special situations. Everyone knew I was a special situation.

That first year I was a therapy student, I had a scholarship, awarded to me based on financial need and academic performance. When I returned to the program with my husband and son in the fall of 1970 as a second-year therapy student, I was informed by letter that my scholarship money was no longer available. No explanation. I found out fifteen months later why my scholarship was not renewed at a graduation party one of the instructors hosted in her home. She was the only married female professor in the program and I liked her so I asked, "Why was my scholarship taken away? My grades were good. And my financial need was greater when I returned with a baby in the fall of my second year."

"When you told us you were pregnant, the other faculty members thought you wouldn't finish the program. I didn't agree, but the majority ruled."

For Frank and me, there was no question regarding my return to school to complete my degree in the fall, with Sam in tow. And I never questioned Frank's need to further his education. Since we both knew I would resume my studies in physical therapy, Frank applied to graduate school at Ohio State University. When the Mechanical Engineering Department at Ohio State University offered him a stipend, he accepted. We both believed in education. Baby or no, we'd make it happen. My parents did not approve.

"How are you going to go to school and take care of a baby? You know, your father and I are not going to help you."

I responded, "Yes, I know," but I thought, *Financially, you haven't provided for me, even before I was pregnant.*

A fiercely independent couple, we achieved academic, career, and family success. I finished my bachelor of science degree in physical therapy in December 1971. Frank completed his master's degree in mechanical engineering at the same time. He accepted a job offer as design and development engineer at Ford Engineering in Dearborn, Michigan. Ford Motor Company paid for our move to Michigan. That state and the Detroit suburbs have been our home ever since.

When we arrived in Michigan, our first abode was a duplex that was so close to Frank's job, he sometimes rode his new Raleigh racing bike with the sewn-up tires to work.

My first job came later, after we settled a bit, after I passed the Michigan Physical Therapy license exam. In the fall of 1972, after Samuel turned two, I was able to work three days per week at Oakwood Hospital. Samuel went to daycare nearby, where he could play and be with other kids. I lucked out with that daycare mom. She seemed to care as much about Sam as she did her own children.

I always picked Samuel up. Those days, everyone assumed I was a nurse. The physical therapy profession was still young, and I was required to wear a white uniform.

On my days off, I enjoyed doing mommy stuff with Sam. I walked to the nearby stores, pulling Samuel behind in a red wagon, or I rode my bike with him on the back. Our outings were to the Montgomery Ward's on one corner, an Italian bakery and a local butcher shop on another.

Frank and I accomplished a lot within those two years after we graduated. We secured jobs, bought a new house, moved into the suburbs, and hooked up with a decorator. We planned the carpet, paint, and wallpaper for our home even before we moved in. And Frank studied for and passed the Law School Admissions Test (LSAT).

For many couples, a family pattern evolves when their first child arrives.

For many couples, a family pattern evolves when their first child arrives. The pattern for our family emerged, after we were in our new home, while Frank was at law school. He worked a full-time job during the day, attended law school at nights, and studied on weekends. I managed the home and parenting. I told Frank where to show up and when. He made his obligatory appearance, as good dads do. That pattern continues today.

Frank proclaims he is a workaholic and proud of it. His addiction to work is approved by our culture. I view his work addiction as an egotistical vehicle that glorifies his role of family breadwinner. Before he took the LSAT, we were more of a unit. Together, we focused on our educations and our future. During those law school years, I believe he acquired a lifelong habit of finding fulfillment outside of his relationship with me, outside of the family. Often, I have felt like an accessory to his pursuits, an essential ingredient to the family mix, a piece of the family package that is labeled "success."

I was pregnant with our second son, Brad, while Frank was in law school. I waited until Brad was four and until Frank was established as an attorney before I again returned to work part-time. My career pursuits always took the back seat. But I didn't mind.

I felt blessed that I'd found physical therapy, a profession where I had the best of both worlds. I could easily find part-time work that sustained my mental needs while at the same time offered a schedule that accommodated my children's lives. I felt I had a life outside the home and adequate time to devote to family life.

My specialty in pediatric physical therapy is the reason I went to graduate school. My basic degree hadn't given me enough information about children's bodies. I needed to better understand how children develop and what interferes with that development.

Basic physical therapy challenged my physical and mental energies. Pediatric therapy challenged my spiritual and emotional energies. In those years, I thrived as I developed my basic mothering instincts. I also delighted in nurturing the progress of my young patients and the development of my own children.

GENTLE POINTS

- We all have the potential to change life's challenges into opportunities for growth.

- Our spiritual growth progresses as we learn life's lessons.

- When we meet obstacles on our physical journey, we choose how to meet those obstacles: we may choose to go around, to go through, or to jump over them. We may even choose to walk the other way and avoid the obstacle altogether.

- Our primitive brain would have us turn away from new patterns of thinking and doing. Like an old shoe, our traditional patterns and old habits are more comfortable than a new pair of shoes.

- Our rational, cognitive brain assimilates new information that can guide us to think outside cultural norms and outdated thinking patterns.

CHAPTER EIGHT
My Children's Childhood

The first home Frank and I bought resembled my childhood home. It was a small ranch in the suburbs of a big city. I felt comfortable as I planted our new family's suburban roots. I cultivated the role of homemaker, tended the challenges and delights of motherhood, and sowed the seeds of relationships.

Even as a young mom, though, I felt like I was a round peg in a square hole in my community. I now realize I have always been a woman with much passion who lives among women who strive to be steadfast and loyal to the patriarchal system we've been born into. I tried to fit into the patriarchal standards and rules.

We lived on a great street for two young boys. The homes were built with sidewalks that curved and sloped and connected every home, with natural ramps for anything on wheels. The boys and I lived there during a time when kids played outside, ran between homes, and knocked on doors to see if a friend could come out to play. The front yards resonated daily with the sounds of wheels against pavement. While the front yard was full of mobility, the backyards held natural playscapes, opportunities for travel and adventure. A creek coursed behind the yards of the houses across the street.

Frank and I finished the basement of this first home. We designed

Brad, my happy, healthy, and bright son who was connected to family, friends, school, pets, and athletics.

six hundred square feet of open play space, bought and installed blue paneled walls, laid a sub-floor, and purchased carpet left over from the auto shows. We installed brackets and shelves along an entire wall, which held the boys' toys. When we bought furniture for the master bedroom, I kept the old double mattress and box spring for the boys to jump on downstairs. It was better than a trampoline. In that neighborhood, we not only had the biggest backyard, we also had the best basement.

Our sons loved playing with TinkerToys—huge plastic tubes of long, short, and medium lengths, with plastic connectors and round disks. Frank and I were often entertained by the boys treating us to a TinkerToy music concert. We clapped and clapped, and during their first performance, I cried.

Later in life, Brad asked me why I had cried.

"Brad, those concerts represented all that was right, all that I strived for as your mom. I was so happy that two brothers could share and shape something together. It meant so much to me that you built and sang music out of plastic. I felt like I had given you boys an opportunity to express yourselves in a fun way. I felt a moment of parent success."

As the years progressed, Frank and I made more money, allowing us to move to a slightly bigger home two miles away. When I remember this second house, it brings memories of a time of change and growth—a coming-of-age period with a traumatic ending.

During these years, Frank, our sons, and I grew out of childhood into adolescence. We solidified our family's personality as upper-middle-class Americans with a strong work ethic. We traveled from innocence into turmoil.

We traveled from innocence into turmoil.

When we first moved in, Brad was in the fifth grade and played baseball. He rode his bicycle on a dirt road to get back and forth to practice. That May, he was thrown from his bike when he hit a rock and fell onto his left arm. He sustained a simple fracture that put him in a cast for four weeks and put his career as a pitcher and batter to rest for that season. As it turned out, his baseball career ended forever, but not due to that left arm injury.

It happened in June, shortly after school let out, maybe even the first day of summer vacation. I worked part-time in a pediatric head injury unit. Brad asked if his friend Luke could sleep over. Frank agreed to it, even though we both had to leave for work in the morning. He felt the boys were old enough to take care of themselves. When Frank left for work that morning, the boys were fine. They insisted that they could get their own breakfast and decided to make scrambled eggs. In the process, Brad's wrist was slashed. Seventeen tendons, two arteries, and the nerves were severed—sliced in half. Brad could have lost his hand. Neighbors took him to the hospital, his hand dangling by threads and wrapped in a towel. Frank and I met them at the hospital.

The surgeon was optimistic when he came out. He said the prognosis was good, that he was able to reattach everything. He said the tight towel saved Brad's hand, but Brad would need lots of therapy. We were told that Brad couldn't use his hand for four weeks. I volunteered to be Brad's physical therapist.

In the hours and days and weeks and years following Brad's hand injury, my thin skin was bruised. Guilt tortured me. Brad's physical and emotional pain became mine. But I had to be strong. I dared not let my anxieties show. I needed to be available for my son. I felt

Brad could have lost his hand. Guilt tortured me.

it imperative that I be a source of steadfast positive thinking, that I put on a take-charge persona that would enable us to move forward. I needed to be Brad's source of healing. I would be a therapist who provided the best therapy possible, who would rehabilitate my son's right hand. I wanted to provide the strongest mothering possible so I could mend the pieces of his spirit that must have been severed along with those structures in his wrist. I had to do it all.

Since I felt so guilty, I quit my job and took a very part-time position at a local therapist's office so I could be close to home, yet still work. I understood myself well enough to know that I could die of the emotional pain if I remained at home 24/7. I would have spiraled into full depression given my son's ruined summer.

Inside, I felt the knife that sliced my son's hand.

By early July, the doctor indicated the tendons had healed enough to begin gentle, passive therapy. My heart cried each day as I removed Brad's splint and the attached wires. Gently, I flexed and extended each and every joint of my son's fingers. Passively, I moved his wrist up and down, side to side. In silence, I swallowed the chasm of screams I heard from the black sutures and swollen incision on his wrist. I assumed a stoic appearance on the outside, as I moved the structures of Brad's hand. Inside, I felt the knife that sliced my son's hand.

Brad's right hand was the outward evidence of a lesion within our family. It was positioned in this outrigger affair of wires, gauze, and sutures. And another invisible wound brewed within.

Sam's adolescent behaviors were huge. He was belligerent and argumentative. He spent as little time at home as possible. In turn, I avoided him as best I could. I consciously tried to protect Brad's fragile recovery from Sam's flamboyant, "I know everything about everything, and you people are just a bunch of idiots" attitude. Male pubescent acting-out behavior was exacerbated in Sam as a result of his secretive alcohol and marijuana use. I'd felt besieged by his rudeness on our last vacation the year before to Yellowstone and the Grand Canyon.

I took some pictures that summer of Brad with his injured hand, but he couldn't smile. What twelve-year-old who had lost his hand the first day of vacation could smile? I didn't want to force happiness, and I didn't want to see my own sadness reflected back in the camera lens. The result is that I have few photos of our family after that summer. I put the camera away for years.

I put the camera away for years.

In September, Brad began middle school with a functional right hand. He did not want me to say anything to the teachers about his injury. But the second day of school, I went to the office anyway. I met with the vice principal and explained what had happened. I asked her to communicate this message to all his teachers:

"Brad sustained a serious right hand injury over the summer. His handwriting skills are still impaired, so he may need some exceptions, such as using a typewriter or the computer for some assignments."

I don't know if that message was ever conveyed. Later that fall, one of his teachers wrote across the top of an assignment,

"*Handwriting terrible. Consider using a typewriter.*"

"Brad," I said, "didn't you tell her about your hand?'

"No."

Not until the winter of 2007 was I in a place where I could let go of guilt and found the peace that comes with a job well done. In my perpetual hunt to recapture the past, I uncovered physical evidence of my son's victories during his middle school years. Not snapshots but something more valuable. I found his writings from that time. I found his thoughts. I saw that he had climbed the mountain after that injury. As I came upon awards and notes, newspaper clippings, and, most precious of all, Brad's own words, I felt like I'd discovered precious gems. His concept of himself during that traumatic period lay nestled among saved schoolwork.

Brad received the Middle School Achievement Award for an outstanding report card in November 1985, five months after the hand injury. The following June, he was an honor student, and he received

These gems validated my son's triumph over his injury and freed me of self-reproach.

a state award for achieving a perfect score on the Michigan Educational Assessment Program. He also received a Recognition Award from the Midwest Talent Search.

These gems not only validated Brad's triumph over his injury, they also freed me of self-reproach. I realized that once he reached the top of the mountain, he shed the baggage of grief so he could move on. I gathered this as I'd ask people who'd met Brad later in his life, "Did you know Brad had a severe hand injury when he was twelve?" They always answered, "No, he never mentioned it."

A few times I had asked, "Brad, does your hand ever bother you?"

He'd reply, "Once in a while. My last two fingers tingle, like if it's going to rain. Sometimes my hand gets tired. Like if I've jammed for a long time."

Brad's autobiography, written in seventh grade, clued me in. When I chose to write this book, I was compelled to read Brad's seventh grade journal. I'm glad I did, because his words brought me peace. My son held my hand as I trekked up the peak of pain and journeyed back in time. Now Brad walks beside me every day, and memories emerge without guilt. I am able to drop the burdens of what a mother *should* do. Instead, I look for life's lessons in what has happened and I celebrate what I *can* do.

My Life Story
WOW
By Brad
[excerpt]

From Page 1.................birth – age Five

I don't actually remember being born, but I know that I was born in Sinai Hospital on February 4ᵗʰ, 1974. I first lived on Dover Drive, a small street with a lot of action. My best friend when I was small was Jerome. He lived three houses down from me and we always got into a lot of trouble. Aaron was my other friend and we got into even more trouble. The first Christmas I remember was when I was three years old. I remember waking up really early and waking everyone else up while I was hiding in the garbage can. We had a great basement in our house because it had no breakables or anything to get into trouble with. Once I took a hammer and hit my brother on the head and he had to get stitches because I hit him so hard. My favorite toys were matchbox cars and Star Wars figures

Page 2......................school to 5th grade

My favorite teacher was Mrs. K. because she did great activities like raising Monarch butterflies and other great projects. I used to want to get homework because my brother always got it. (Sam is now sixteen.) Years five and six for me were fun because I got interested in sports. I really liked soccer and was pretty good at it. Baseball was also fun. Basketball became my center of interest at age seven. When I was eight we moved to a secluded Main Street house, and I had to make new friends. The summer we moved was fun because I started getting interested in swimming and we joined our local swim club. Also I got a bunch of firecrackers and I had a real bash with those. I started playing marbles in fifth grade and got pretty good at them. My grandfather worked at a factory and he got me some gigantic steelies which I won zillions of marbles with.

Fifth grade summer for me was crummy in the beginning and great at the end. In the beginning we went to the Grand Canyons and Las Vegas which was way too hot for me. At the end, we came home and I had a great summer. (Any summer without school is great!)

Following is what Brad wrote about the year of his hand injury:

My sixth grade school year was great. I really learned a lot and had quite a bit of fun. I became interested in computers because my mom and dad had purchased an IBM PC. I got tons of games and loved it. One thing I really liked was I learned to type well. (That is how I am *doing this report!) That summer was great too. It was great weather and I enjoyed it.*

Page 4......................7th grade and closing

> *His words brought me peace.*

I can definitely say I have enjoyed my life as my parents have helped, along with my brother and other people. If I could live it over I would do the same things I have done.

Brad's words blew me away, to a good space. My son's words taught me to forgive myself, to have compassion for me, and to accept myself for doing the best I knew how to do at that time.

Brad's death and his hand injury were not the only devastating experiences I faced as a mother. Sam also contributed to the challenges I have been required to face in this life.

Gentle Points

- Memories of our deceased children become the most precious gifts we have of their life.

- Guilt and shame and pain are barriers to retrieving our precious memories.

- The most valuable person we need to forgive in life is ourselves.

CHAPTER NINE

Problems

I suspected something was wrong with Sam, and I feared drugs were involved. When I'd question him, he would yell, "Leave me alone. You don't know what you're talking about!"

"Sam, where were you last night? I know you were drinking. I can smell it on you."

"I'm fine. Don't you have anything better to do than go around smelling people?"

I saw the furtive demeanor of my oldest son, but my instincts were muzzled. My observations were rejected and dismissed by Frank. I tried to keep the family peace as best I could. Somehow, both Sam and his dad had a way of throwing the blame back on me whenever I expressed my concerns.

Sam's behavior was obvious to me, but not to his dad. Perhaps it is easier for males to ignore things that make them uncomfortable. Especially feelings. By nature and nurture, I believe men avoid feelings; the male energy tends to dismiss, ignore, bury, or get angry rather than deal with them. I

Traditional behavioral intervention programs don't work when a family member is a substance abuser.

disciplined Sam the best I knew how. He wrote hundreds of "I must not use profanity" and "I must not call names" sentences. Later, I'd assign him five-hundred-word essays on "Why I should be nice to my brother" or "How I can show respect to my mother." We saw counselors during that time, which helped only me feel like we were doing something. Really, all counseling did was put a few Band-aids on our family's wounds. The real disease was Sam's addiction.

What I learned later was that traditional behavioral intervention programs don't work when a family member is a substance abuser. Much of Sam's outrageous adolescent behaviors were driven by a developing addiction to marijuana and alcohol. That was why he didn't like to be at our house, why he didn't want to tell us where he was going, why he came home after curfew, why he resented my asking him questions, and why he was mean and surly to his brother. When I expressed my concern for what was happening, I got in the way of his addiction. He needed to hide from me and from his brother. He didn't want Brad to snitch on him.

Subconsciously, maybe, I thought a move would provide a geographic cure to our family disharmony. Deep down, perhaps I felt a new home could bring our family a new lifestyle. Besides, there's nothing like building a home to distract a person from the daily dysfunctions. Consciously, Frank and I looked at building a home as an opportunity. We had sufficient income as Frank was now an established attorney with the promise of becoming a partner, and I worked part-time for a therapist in town.

We moved into the new home we built in the spring of 1988, a few months before Sam graduated from high school. Maybe that move did keep Sam's alcohol and marijuana use at bay, or maybe it just gave Frank and me enough distractions so we felt like a functional, focused family for awhile.

After Sam graduated from high school, as we settled into our routines, I expected our family would have order—a renewed family life—that Sam would come home every night, that he would honor his curfew, and that he would be pleasant around his family. But we soon found that nothing had changed.

By the end of June that year, my reverie about our family shattered. At any given moment, we had no idea where Sam was or whom he was with. Our house was a place for him to crash at will. One evening, Frank and I discussed Sam's options with him calmly. We told him he either needed to comply with our rules for decent family living or he could move out. He chose to move out. That night, he went to live with a friend in the loft of their barn. I learned later that the friend's mother was told by Sam that he wasn't getting along with his parents. I would have thought she'd have called us. To this day, I'm not sure where he stayed or which friend it was. Sam continued to work, and he did come by to see us occasionally. By summer's end, we'd worked out a reasonable solution. Sam still wanted to attend college in the fall and realized he needed us for tuition support.

Sam went to Philadelphia for his first year of college. Then he transferred to a Michigan school where he lived on campus. During those years, it was just Frank, Brad, and me at home. They should have been smooth years. Years to settle down and enjoy our easy-going, connected second son who loved sports and computers, made friends easily, and was as smart and talented as his brother, but in different ways and without the edginess. With Sam's intensity out of the way, I thought we'd be a happy threesome.

Brad started high school the fall Sam left, but he wasn't himself. He still hung with his old friends, but he also acquired friendships with kids we didn't know. Frank and I were concerned about these kids. We didn't know them or their parents. Brad joined the cross country team and, with my persistence, went to cross country camp. But he seemed distant and remote.

Brad was disconnected because he had started doing drugs and was drinking. For Brad, my feminine sensitivities were buried under my guilt. Since my mother's intuition with Sam's behavior had been disregarded, I learned to bury the concerns I had about Brad.

Brad's music tastes had evolved into heavy metal, AC/DC, Jimi Hendrix, and the Grateful Dead. He even went with a friend to a

Grateful Dead concert in Chicago. He stayed with Frank's aunt, who was happy to provide lodging for her nephew's son.

Nobody but me seemed concerned that wanting to follow the Grateful Dead around for the rest of your life was not a good thing.

Nobody but me seemed concerned that wanting to follow the Grateful Dead around for the rest of your life was not a good thing. Frank thought I was just a worrywart like my mom. He told me I was trying to control Brad instead of just letting him do what he wanted. After all, Brad was a good kid and he didn't give us a hard time like Sam had.

I told Frank, "Something's not right. Brad doesn't communicate. I don't know these friends he hangs with. I don't know the parents. One minute he's jamming in someone's garage, the next he wants to go to Cleveland for some kind of Dungeons and Dragons thing. He doesn't play sports anymore. I don't understand why he didn't try out for the high school soccer team. He was always so good at soccer. Or the basketball team. When he played basketball for the Rec Center, he was practically the star of every team. I know he'd be great, but he doesn't even want to try out."

"Maybe he's just not interested. Don't push him," replied Frank.

"I'm not pushing him, I'm concerned. The healthiest thing he does is that fantasy baseball, when he brings those guys like Jim and Tim and Ron over. Those kids are into academics, healthy stuff. I know their parents."

"His grades are good," Frank commented.

"I know his grades are good. That's just it. They're good, not great. He hardly ever studies. Imagine what he could do if he put in some effort. He could do better, but he doesn't care. He's floating, just getting by. I don't know if he's depressed. He hardly talks to us." I continued to express my concerns.

"Brad's fine. You worry too much. Stop trying to control him," was Frank's reply.

Brad's answer to my inquiries and concerns was, "You're comparing me to Sam. I'm not Sam."

"Brad, I'm not comparing you to Sam. I'm trying to encourage you to be all that you can be," I told him.

In the spring of 1992, Frank and I went to California for a four-day trip while my parents stayed with Brad at home. Brad went to a homecoming dance. My parents were called by school officials, as Brad was involved with reports of drinking. When we came home, Brad lay on the white loveseat in our kitchen, picking at his eyelashes.

I asked him, "What's wrong with your eye?" and he said, "Nothing."

Later, Brad told us he'd done LSD and that he had images that crackled behind his eyeballs. The eyelash picking, that homecoming report, and his overall disconnected behavior pushed me into action. I found a psychiatrist.

The first psychiatrist Brad saw was Dr. Herod, the recently retired director of the regional child psychiatric facility. Child psychiatric residents and psychology interns trained under him. The doctor's credentials were outstanding. We felt we were in competent, professional hands.

Brad saw Dr. Herod for about six months during his junior year. During that time, his erratic behaviors increased. His marijuana use escalated. He stole the keys to Frank's Thunderbird and got into an accident. He withdrew more from social activities. He hung with new friends—kids with long hair, shuffling gaits, and unkempt appearances. He stayed up late on the computer. Frank had to drag him out of bed in the mornings and drive him to school. Dr. Herod never suggested a meeting with Frank and me. Whenever we asked how Brad was doing, he reminded us that he had a confidentiality agreement with our son.

Whenever we asked how Brad was doing, Dr. Herod reminded us that he had a confidentiality agreement with our son.

"I can only tell you if I see behaviors that threaten Brad's life or the life of others."

"Do you mean to say that we, his parents, who pay your bills, cannot know what's going on with our dependent fifteen-year-old?" I asked.

"The fact that he's a teenager is all the more reason why I can't divulge patient-doctor information. I want Brad to trust me, feel free to tell me anything, not worry that I'm going to snitch on him. If I thought his life was in danger, I would tell you," replied the doctor.

"What do you call taking our car without permission, without having a driver's license, and getting into an accident?" asked Frank.

"That's just normal teenage behavior. Have his grades dropped?"

"No, they haven't dropped, but they're not as good as he is capable of," I replied.

"Has he threatened either of you or himself with bodily harm?" asked Dr. Herod.

"No," we replied.

"I didn't think so. Brad is a normal adolescent, experimenting a little, trying to find where he fits in. He may be a little immature. Mom, I think you're overprotective. Maybe you need to back off a little."

No parent wants to believe there's anything wrong with their kid. It was easier to accept the doctor's words that we were overly concerned parents, that our son was immature, and that he would be fine. This was not the last time we would hear this diagnosis.

Gentle Points

- Pay attention to that voice in your heart.

- The traditional handmaiden idea—the woman's place in the lovely family home—can be a barrier to our instinctive voice, which is our mother's, father's, or our intuition.

- Life is a balance between rational, mental energy and honoring the voice of our heart and soul, the seat of our emotional and spiritual energies.

CHAPTER TEN

Beginning Signs
of Mental Illness

The summer Brad was a senior in high school, Sam was a senior at the university. It was the same summer that Frank's niece, Amy, destined to become Scott's mom, stayed with us for a few weeks. I was thrilled. I'd always wanted a girl, and we had plenty of room in the home we'd built. The boys each had a large bedroom upstairs, plus there was another bedroom with its own bathroom. I'd originally finished that area with the idea that someday Frank and I would move our master suite upstairs, in the event that our parents or an elderly aunt might need to live with us. It was perfect for a girl. I had wallpapered the room with a mauve and black vine pattern and the carpet was a soft mauve. Amy's parents also liked the idea of her living with us. She'd become a handful for them. Similar to Sam, she didn't like following rules or having a curfew.

I was not so naïve to think Amy asked to stay with us because she wanted to bond with me. I imagined she wanted to meet boys, my sons' friends, which I thought was great. I hoped her presence would be a catalyst for teenage gatherings at our home. I was wrong. I believe now that Amy picked our family because she knew our boys did drugs, and she figured she could party with them.

Amy's stay with us went well. We didn't argue. We were all quite cordial. I was busy with my Child Life Therapy practice. Physically challenged children and their families came and went through a separate clinic entrance in the lower level of my home. I kept Amy busy with various jobs that were on my back burner, like painting outdoor furniture and tending flower beds. She helped with meal preparation. Sam was more settled by then. He worked in landscaping, and Brad worked at a restaurant. All three of them worked together on one big project in our yard. It was Sam's idea. Under his direction, they landscaped several beds with rocks and boulders. On weekends and late afternoons, they hauled up to a thousand rocks from a nearby quarry. They filled one bed entirely with rocks so it looked like a bumpy pond, with tall pines in the background. I don't know how much partying they did, but they did leave a wonderful legacy of boulder landscaping at our home.

I was excited to plan some outings that I could share with a girl, like church and cultural events. But we only did this once. We rode the People Mover in Detroit and toured the renovated Fox Theatre. Amy was not enthusiastic about anything I planned, but at least she didn't complain or act sullen, like the boys did.

Overall, like Sam, Brad seemed more settled that summer. He was due to graduate from high school and planned to major in computer engineering. He only talked about going to Arizona State University because it was warm there. He didn't want to look at any other colleges. I hoped that during the school year he'd become more open-minded, and we could look at colleges closer to home.

As fall began, Brad's old friends, the ones whose parents I knew, came to our house and played fantasy baseball and congregated around the computer. But I had that old gut feeling return as the school year progressed. I always worried about Brad, even though everyone told me there was nothing to worry about and there were no specific disturbances. Even when I attended his cross country meets, my son seemed out of sync.

I thought, *Maybe I'm the one who's not connected. Maybe there is something wrong with me. I must be lousy at mothering teenage sons.*

There were three counselors at Brad's high school—two academic advisors and another one named Charlie. I gathered Charlie was available for students with problems, kids coming out of rehab, maybe kids with special needs. We'd been to Brad's parent-teacher conference in October where his teachers gave us these nice reports. We even met with his academic advisor, who indicated I needn't be concerned. Brad's grades were fine; he wouldn't have any trouble getting into college.

Then, one day in November, a few weeks after the parent-teacher conference, Charlie called me. He told me that Brad had a lot of absences from school and was often late to class. He said some of the other students had come to him expressing concern about Brad's use.

Absences? Late? Use of what? Mr. Charlie, why hasn't anyone told me this before?

He told me that he'd met with Brad, and then he asked me if I knew Brad was getting high every day.

"No," I said. I was shocked. Stunned.

Charlie told me that he believed Brad's use was so severe that outpatient treatment probably wouldn't work. He recommended we place Brad in an inpatient rehab program over Christmas break. While everything Charlie said made sense, I was dumbfounded. How could Brad have seen Dr. Herod for all those months the year before and there was never a word said about treatment for "chemical dependence" or "inpatient rehab" or "substance abuse"? Charlie's terms were new to me.

Frank and I took Charlie's recommendation and made plans to send Brad to a hospital that provided inpatient, outpatient, and assessment services for adults and adolescents with chemical dependency.

The only treatment for chemical dependency is abstinence.

Addiction—or chemical dependency—is labeled a disease. The only treatment for this disease is abstinence. The twelve-step process is typically used in the recovery treatment. I never thought I'd need chemical dependency treatment for my son, a high school senior. We were supposed to be planning his college future, not seeking treatment for substance abuse.

While planning for Brad's treatment, I seized the opportunity to express and stand firm with my concerns about Sam. When Frank and I threatened Sam with holding back college tuition unless he went to rehab also, Sam admitted he was deep into his addiction. Both sons went into rehab at the same time. I told my parents we would not be traveling over Christmas. For the first time in our married lives, we wouldn't be in Cleveland or Pennsylvania for the holidays. Sam and Brad were in rehab.

You know the family life you hoped for has ended when both of your sons are in rehab and you spend Christmas Day gluing strips of wallpaper in your teenage son's bedroom. While I glued, Frank consulted with the staff in the adult wing of the rehab center. They wanted to kick Sam out, as he defied some of their rules. After negotiating terms for Sam to stay, Frank went to the juvenile side of rehab, where Brad was also a patient.

Since everything else around me was out of control, I decided to hang wallpaper on Christmas Day in 1991. This was something I could control. I could not visit my sons and pretend to be happy and jolly. I'd been at rehab every day following their admission. I attended all the family therapy sessions, the group meetings, and all of the optional and required programs possible. The hospital hadn't planned anything for Christmas Day. They told families they could order and pay for an extra meal. I couldn't stomach the idea of eating cafeteria food on Christmas Day with a forced smile. The gift I could give Brad that year was to finish the wallpaper in his room.

By that Christmas, Frank and I had hung lots of wallpaper. I often related to friends and family how that was one area of our marriage where we functioned superbly together. Many couples argue and fight over this undertaking. Frank and I argued over lots of things, but we worked well as a team when it came to hanging wallpaper. I was able to paper a wall of Brad's bedroom by myself, using the remnants I'd saved from the rest of the walls. That last wall was unfinished because there

Since everything else around me was out of control, I decided to hang wallpaper on Christmas Day.

hadn't been enough paper to finish it. Like a puzzle, I fit the fragments together. I was glad to be productive that day. I did something with my hands, something for Brad.

My sons completed their twenty-one days of inpatient stay. Frank and I learned way more than we ever wanted to know about substance abuse, the twelve-step program, and the symptoms of dependency, co-dependency, and enabling. Sam returned to his studies and received his college degree that June. The hospital directed him to follow up his treatment by attending Alcoholics Anonymous or Narcotics Anonymous meetings several times per week. Maybe Sam attended a meeting or two, but it is in his nature to resist rules and rebel against authority. He believes he knows what's best for him.

Meanwhile back at home, our focus was on Brad, who still lived with us. We were desperate to help and guide him into the future. When a problem hits Frank and me in the face, we charge ahead and do everything in our power to fix it. We develop plans. First born, we'd always been the responsible son, daughter, student, citizen, and parent. We attended parent support meetings at the hospital and Al-Anon meetings in the community. We did our assigned homework and got rid of all of the liquor in our house. We told my parents that we wouldn't serve alcohol in our home anymore. We discussed and we argued about when we saw enabling and codependent behaviors in each other. Our learning curve was high.

Brad entered his outpatient rehab recovery with commitment. He connected to the twelve-step promise: Stay clean, work the program, and you'll feel better. He, too, attended meetings in the community and made new friends, other teenagers recovering from substance abuse. These were delightful friends, friends who seemed to enjoy coming to our home. He found a sponsor. He attended the outpatient sessions at the hospital and read the AA book. Brad's learning curve soared next to ours.

Imagine my surprise when we were told by a hospital counselor that Brad wasn't working a very good program. The counselor suggested that Brad was still using. Brad swore he wasn't. He told the counselor he didn't hang with friends that used drugs and alcohol anymore. The counselor pointed out that Brad did not participate in the group activities and still seemed withdrawn.

Brad explained that he didn't participate fully because he didn't feel the peace and tranquility he was supposed to get from the First Step of the twelve step program. He felt betrayed and confused. Rehab wasn't working, and we couldn't figure out why.

A GENTLE POINT

- Sometimes...perhaps all the time...the pursuit of peace of mind is our only guide.

CHAPTER ELEVEN

Mental Illness Journey

Our journey into mental illness officially began in June 1992, two weekends before Brad was expected to graduate from high school. Brad's inner turmoil came outward. He couldn't hide his symptoms. During this journey, we were placed into positions where we needed to decide the risks and benefits of our choices. Like my patients' parents, I searched for clinics, doctors, programs, and medications.

On one of those rare nights when Sam attended a local AA meeting with his brother, a friend of Brad's accompanied him home and took us aside. The friend told us he was worried about Brad. He said everyone at the meeting thought Brad was still *Our journey into mental illness officially began two weekends before our son was to graduate from high school.* using drugs because Brad acted strange at the meeting. Brad thought people were talking about him, were plotting to kill him, that they said weird things about him. He'd even stood up and told everyone to shut up and leave him alone. Brad swore to his friend that he was clean, and his friend believed him. The next morning, Sam confirmed that he thought his brother was acting strange.

That Friday night in June, Brad sat in a recliner in the family room and screamed at Frank and me. He wanted us to leave him alone; he just wanted to die. He wanted to jump through the glass doors and be done with it. His head hurt, he couldn't stand it anymore. We called EMS. My gorgeous son, bright, handsome, athletic, and tenderhearted beyond any male I'd ever known, with a high school graduation party in the works, wanted to end it all. EMS came with cops. They strapped him to a gurney and hauled him off in an ambulance.

Frank and I followed. When we arrived at the emergency room, a nurse came to us. She said they wanted Brad to stay overnight so they could observe him and that they had given him a shot of Haldol.

"That always calms them down," she said.

Them? Who are them? I thought.

The mentally ill, I learned.

Therapists. Social workers. Substance abuse counselors. Drug rehab. Psychologists. Psychiatrists. Alcoholics Anonymous. Narcotics Anonymous. Families Anonymous. Psych wards. Lockdown wards. Adolescent psychiatric programs. Inpatient treatment. Outpatient treatment. Mental health hospitals. By the end of the summer, we got to know them all.

> *By the time Brad died, he had been treated by eleven psychiatrists.*

By the time Brad died, he had been treated by eleven psychiatrists. Between the ages of sixteen and twenty-one, he'd been evaluated in fourteen treatment centers. The doctors' professional care of my son varied. Some of the psychiatrists only evaluated him and then referred him to a therapist. Some got to know Brad over several days and weeks of inpatient hospitalization. Some *only* prescribed medications, while others *should have* prescribed meds. Some of them consulted with Frank and me about our son, others didn't consult with us at all but should have. In my eyes, of those eleven, four were competent. They were professionals who recognized mental illness when they saw it. Those four doctors knew the importance of psychotropic medications and the necessity of monitoring a patient's response to these medications. Those four physicians understood our son needed not only medical support but his parents' support.

Besides psychiatrists, within and without each treatment facility came a slew of therapists, professionals with social work degrees who provided talk therapy while Brad was an inpatient or an outpatient.

We didn't realize Brad had actually been diagnosed with depression back when he saw Dr. Herod because that psychiatrist never prescribed any medications, nor did he inform Frank and me of the diagnosis. Years later, after Frank accumulated all Brad's medical records, he read Dr. Herod's report, which indicated Brad had "poly-substance abuse" and "self-destructive behaviors." Why hadn't he told us?

After that first emergency room admit, Brad was placed on Haldol and discharged after two days. We were advised to follow up with Dr. Steve, a graduate from the University of Michigan Medical School. Brad saw Dr. Steve for two months. Those months were a roller-coaster ride of hallucinations and depression. A lot of different medications were prescribed and tried, but Brad was never stabilized under this doctor's care.

Dr. Steve misdiagnosed our son with unipolar depression. Due to this diagnosis, he was given Prozac, an antidepressant. This medication had a devastating effect on our son. It caused Brad to have a full-blown mania attack when he and Frank toured an in-state college campus.

On their way home from the college tour, I searched and found another hospital for Frank to take Brad to. During this stay, Brad was under the care of Dr. Felipe. The doctor consulted with us twice, on the first and last day of Brad's twelve inpatient days. Dr. Felipe told us about the medications he'd prescribed for Brad. He began with Navane, which he had to discontinue as it made Brad jittery. Upon discharge, he gave us a prescription for Loxitane and Restoril and pronounced Brad cured.

"Brad should go to college. He needs to be independent, away from the home, so that he can have an opportunity to make his own decisions and realize the consequences of those decisions. Don't overprotect him, Mom," Dr. Felipe told me.

Given the doctor's advice, we were hopeful, but given our son's recent history, we were also scared. We packed Brad up to begin his freshman year at college. I went to the University Health Center and requested a meeting with someone in mental health. I gave Brad's medical history to the psychologist. I asked this doctor to stay in touch with us. However, he didn't communicate with me unless I called him and set up an appointment. The college mental health professionals did prescribe various medications, but Brad remained depressed and withdrawn, had difficulty with eye contact, and had ongoing hallucinations. No one told me about these symptoms.

Somehow, Brad survived that freshman year and completed his academics successfully with a 3.3 grade point average.

The summer of 1993 progressed relatively smoothly. But things changed as Brad entered his sophomore year of college. My memories of Brad's last days in that college town are of him roaming the lockdown ward of the local hospital's psychiatric wing, while Frank and I packed his college gear in the back of our car. We knew Brad would not be returning to school there. In September 1993, his mania had exploded.

This full-blown manic episode occurred in his college apartment. His roommate's parents called us, and we went to take care of him. When we arrived, the apartment's appearance could have been a typical college boys' bachelor pad, except for Brad, who embodied chaos. He pranced around like a wild stallion. Oblivious to social amenities, he approached the parents and his peers alike, in their face. With nostrils flared, a gush of words came out. He paraded into the kitchen, opened a can of soup, slurped it, and spilled it on the carpet as he bounced around the living room. He grabbed his electric guitar, plugged it in, and smiled as he threw the guitar behind his back, playing a heavy metal tune, humming and gyrating at the same time. At one point, he picked up a spray mist deodorizer, smiled, and sprayed one of the mothers near her face. Her husband almost attacked Brad, but then backed off.

He said to Frank, "I can see things are not normal."

"I really feel sorry for you and your wife," said one of the mothers.

Eventually, everyone vacated the apartment, except Brad and Frank. Brad held his ground. He planned to stay. Frank called me. I had remained in the car with my portable phone. Frank wanted to leave Brad there by himself. "He'll have to learn a lesson from this. He'll have to fend for himself."

"No. We can't leave him. He's sick. We have to get help. I've been calling around to find someplace to take him." Frank and I plotted what we would do in order to get Brad to the emergency room again.

"He's sick. We have to get help," I pleaded with my husband.

An hour later, Frank called. "Okay, Brad agreed to get something to eat. We'll be outside the apartment in fifteen minutes."

We drove straight to the hospital emergency room. I had called ahead, so the hospital expected us, with the caveat, "We won't be able to admit him unless he cooperates. You need a court order if he's to be admitted against his will."

In the waiting room, Brad paced. He jumped in and out of chairs, and inside and outside the room. People stared. He wanted out. He wasn't going to cooperate. We'd tricked him, and he was angry. As calmly as possible, we edged him closer and closer to the intake person and cajoled him into the interview room. Within minutes, three attendants restrained and escorted Brad into a room where he was given a shot of Haldol.

While Brad was being subdued, we were surprised when a social worker came in to meet with us on a Sunday night. She sought information from us regarding Brad's history. No other social worker had ever asked us for our son's history. After several rounds of questions, we were informed that Brad was having a manic episode. This was the first time we'd heard the word manic. The social worker told us Brad had been assigned to Dr. Bausch.

We met Dr. Bausch the next day. Solid, as his German name suggested, he was a stocky, middle-aged man with a square face and brown hair, dressed in a white lab coat. Glasses framed his serious, yet compassionate, eyes.

"I believe your son has bipolar disorder," Dr. Bausch told us. "Are you familiar with this term?"

"Is that the same as manic depression?" we asked.

"Yes. Manic depression is the old term. The medical community has switched to bipolar, so as to differentiate the condition from depression, which is unipolar. I brought this medical book, the *DSM-III-R*, sort of the bible for doctors. I think it will help if I read the definition of *bipolar* to you. 'A patient whose history of mania is severe enough to require hospitalization, usually accompanied by psychotic features. The essential feature of a Manic Episode is either elevated, expansive, or irritable behavior, severe enough to cause marked impairment in usual social activities or relationships with others, or requires hospitalization to prevent harm to self and others. Associated symptoms include inflated self-esteem or grandiosity, decreased need for sleep, pressure of speech, and flight of ideas.' Does any of this make sense to you?"

"Doctor, you just described our son's behavior for the past couple of years. Why haven't we been told this before?"

"Your son has a lifelong illness. He will always need your support. Typically, a person diagnosed as bipolar has a life expectancy of age thirty. No one dies of bipolar, but they are at great risk for suicide, for using poor judgment, and for placing themselves in dangerous situations. Medications, therapy, and family support are the deciding factors for increasing longevity."

"Your son has a lifelong illness. He will always need your support," the doctor told us.

Like train engines, Frank and I emerged from our tunnel of ignorance. Finally, we were fueled with a real diagnosis. Bipolar clarified our son's inexplicable behavior. We had hope. There were medications available. We had means.

We would pay whatever fees. We were capable. We could research all avenues and provide Brad any and all needed therapy. We loved our son. I vowed we would see our son through every bipolar challenge. I would not let him die an early death.

All aboard. Together, Brad, Frank, and I pulled out of the hospital station driving the Bipolar Information Express. We joined the Alliance for the Mentally Ill. We read books written by the renowned, by parents, by patients, by doctors. Our train traveled through towns throughout Michigan, Florida, and Ohio, with side trips into hospitals, clinics, rehab facilities, and adult foster care homes.

The names, dates, titles of health professionals marching in and out of our lives, the numbers of hospitalizations, and the symptoms were unique to my son's mental illness. But the experience is the same for any family who encounters mental illness. Our journeys are always about uncertainty and pain.

We had hope; bipolar clarified our son's inexplicable behavior.

And a woman spoke, saying, "Tell us of Pain."

And he said: "Your pain is the breaking of the shell that encloses your understanding. Even as the stone of the fruit must break, that its heart may stand in the sun, so must you know pain.....Pain is the bitter potion by which the physician within you heals your sick self. Therefore trust the physician. For his hand, though heavy and hard, is guided by the tender hand of the Unseen. And the cup he brings, though it burns your lips, has been fashioned of the clay which the otter has moistened with His own sacred tears" (Kahlil Gibran, *The Prophet* [New York: Knopf, 1991]).

CHAPTER TWELVE
Travel on the
Mental Illness Tracks

When Brad was in the hospital near the college, we finally received a definitive diagnosis. We learned more and more about his behavior. Brad stayed in the hospital for twenty-one days, the maximum number of days our health insurance allowed. Everyone agreed he needed additional treatment in a residential facility. I found a Christian respite center in Grand Rapids. At the time, I thought the center was an answer to our prayers. They provided a day treatment program, in addition to residency, and they were Christian. We set Brad up in a furnished foster care home, where his conduct was monitored by whichever home manager was on assignment for their eight-hour shift. Brad's walk to the scheduled activities and therapies was through pleasant grounds carpeted with pine needles. There was also a hospital on the campus.

Brad was not chemically stable as we headed to Grand Rapids. He was somewhat delusional and not very grounded in reality. He wanted to begin a music career. He talked about earning enough money to buy a telescope so he could look at the stars. After a week's residency, he hadn't unpacked a single item. His alarm clock, pictures, and hygiene items were exactly as I put them, as if glued in place. Within a week, he decompensated. His inappropriate smiling, which I'd seen when he was suicidal, returned. He was admitted to the hospital after ten days in the day program.

In the hospital, Dr. Gray admitted Brad because he was experiencing psychotic symptoms and hearing voices. Along with not unpacking, I don't think Brad had taken a shower, brushed his teeth, or changed his clothes that entire time. Because of the psychosis, Dr. Gray changed all of Brad's medications and warned us, "You know, Brad may not have bipolar. He might be schizophrenic."

His words sounded like a threat. We immediately disliked him. If he knew anything about Brad's medical history, it wasn't because he asked us. Perhaps he read the information we provided when we filled out the forms for the day program admit. I'll never know.

In Grand Rapids Frank and I figured out how to get around the patient confidentiality barrier. Even though we agreed to pay all of our nineteen-year-old dependent son's medical bills, the medical staff would not talk to us. In the prior hospital, we learned if Brad signed a waiver allowing us to talk to medical personnel about his medical care, he relinquished his confidentiality rights. Brad was always willing to sign this waiver. After he signed it, we then walked the waiver to the nurses' station and watched as they placed it in the medical chart. When I'd phone the Grand Rapids hospital to inquire about my son, the staff appeared ignorant of the waiver. They said, "I'm sorry ma'am, I can't talk to you about this person. I can only tell you if they're here or not."

At my next visit, I stood at the nurses' station and watched as they went through the chart, found the waiver, and put it in front so the next day they'd know they could talk to me. I understand that rules are rules, but so often it seems to me patient's rights are more important than the patient. Civil rights and individualism supersede family support in Western medicine. No doubt there's an argument for the other side. I'm sure patient rights have been abused. But that's not our story. In our case, Brad would have been lost without his parents' support and our ability to fight to have our concerned voices heard.

Besides wanting to know how Brad was doing, as any mother wants to know with any illness, it was critical for me to know the details of Brad's medications, the dosage, the symptoms being treated by each drug, and what side effects might occur. I understood the importance of these details, thanks to our previous doctor. Much of the healing for the mentally ill lies in psychopharmacological treatment and in finding the right balance of chemicals that fit the individual's physiological makeup. Healing Brad's mind was not going to happen with talk therapy alone or medical personnel who chose not to rely on his medical history. His neurochemistry was out of whack, and he required heavy-duty chemicals to restore balance.

We only met Dr. Gray once during Brad's two-week stay at the hospital. He kept Brad on Lithium but took him off the Klonopin and Depakote that had been prescribed by Dr. Bausch. Dr. Gray switched him to Trilofan and Artane. When I questioned him about these meds, Dr. Gray assumed one of those "I am the doctor" attitudes, so I'm still unclear what those meds were supposed to do. Frankly, I believe it was malpractice to change the meds of a mentally ill patient so quickly. Brad had only been on Klonopin, Depakote, and Lithium for three weeks. It takes months to evaluate the effects of these antipsychotic meds. Yes, Brad had decompensated while on the campus, but he was cunning and newly diagnosed with a mental disorder. He needed time to adjust. I believe Dr. Gray should have changed one medicine at a time and observed Brad for awhile. Or involve Frank and me: ask us what behavioral changes we saw, positive or negative. Frank and I knew that Brad was not stable at the Grand Rapids place. What we didn't know was what medication and dosages he was actually taking. I was just beginning to learn about blood levels for patients on Lithium, and I had to fight to get this information.

Divine providence sent me a mentor around this time who taught me the importance of psychopharmacology. A nurse in my Bible study class had a son with the same diagnosis as Brad. Her son lived with them and became stable under his parents' watchful eyes. She counseled me during the fall and winter of Brad's decline. She helped me learn the mental health lingo and the language of pharmaceuticals. She explained the importance of blood levels, dosage, and the relationship of medications and behavior. I became a student of mental illness.

Divine providence sent me a mentor.

The last day we saw Brad in Grand Rapids, he seemed worse than when he'd left his prior hospitalization. He was restless, yet he seemed depressed at the same time. He didn't want to talk to us, cared less when we came, and didn't ask us to bring anything except cigarettes. He had just begun to smoke. Yet, after a two-week hospitalization, the doctor discharged him and sent him back to the day program on campus. Something wasn't right.

Brad went AWOL from the day program. On October 27, 1993, Brad walked off that Christian campus. He called a buddy. He convinced his friend and his friend's mother to make the three-hour trip and bring him back to our hometown. Frank and I had no knowledge of his escape. Neither the friend's mother nor anyone from the Christian center called us. That afternoon when we phoned Brad at the day program's foster care house, they told us he'd left.

I prayed with faith, hope, and love.

Frank found him that night, wandering the streets of our hometown. While Frank looked for our son, I sat on the couch praying and pleading with God to guide Frank, direct him to Brad, and bring them home. I prayed with faith, hope, and love. Frank and Brad came home around midnight. My faith in my prayers never wavered that night, but my trust in Christian programs and doctors ended. From that night forward, I evaluated Brad's treatment on the strength of my growing medical knowledge of mental illness and my instincts.

A roller-coaster ride began. Brad was home and mentally unstable with no medications, no doctor, no therapist, and nowhere to go. A job was out of the question. College wasn't even on the radar screen. Our boy was sick. He needed treatment. He needed professional help.

Our next stop was a day program near Ann Arbor. Dr. Z. was psychiatrist number eight. Brad participated in that program from November 3 to November 22. He was kicked out for making inappropriate gestures to one of the girls.

With Brad at home, I was the one who communicated with Dr. Z. He answered my questions and taught me about the medications. Under his care, Brad's Lithium dosage was increased, and his blood serum levels moved into the therapeutic range. Frank and I saw a significant decrease in Brad's manic and psychotic symptoms.

My daily responsibilities became medication distributor and symptom observer. I watched Brad gulp down his medications every day he was under my care. He struggled with their efficacy, he questioned them, and he argued that they didn't do any good, but he took them. Deep down, he understood they might help. We had to try.

That winter, he was stable enough to attend our local community college. Later, we realized Brad not only drove to his classes, he also drove to hang with friends who used street drugs. He had started using again.

Dr. Z. told us this was not uncommon. He said psychotropic medications don't work as fast as street drugs in helping someone feel good and that many mentally ill patients self-medicate. Still, street drugs are dangerous for the mentally ill because their effects on the brain are unknown. Pharmaceutical companies have no interest in studying the effects of marijuana, alcohol, or LSD so the only data and control the medical community has is with prescription drugs.

The doctor did not seem as alarmed about the street drug use as we were. Brad was becoming manic again.

In February 1994, Brad was admitted to another hospital through our county's Psychiatric Intervention Center. He was in the psych ward for a week. By then, we'd become familiar with the term "dual diagnosis." We knew Brad had a mental illness, bipolar disorder, but he also had a substance abuse disorder. We also knew we couldn't treat him at home. He was too clever. We chose not to repeat that particular roller-coaster ride by bringing him home. Although Brad thought we were coming home when he was discharged, we delivered him back to the rehab center where he'd been two years before.

With mental illness, the diagnosed person and family members ride the extreme dips and climbs of the disease. There was a climb of hope every time we started a new program, saw a new therapist or a new doctor, or started a new medicine. When manic, Brad would have these feelings of power, like nothing could stop him, that if he followed the rules, he could overcome anything. He'd be obsessed, have all this energy, be on fire all the time, in constant motion. But then his thoughts spun out of control. He'd be in a group, at a meeting, or at a concert and feel like people were looking at him, nobody liked him, and everyone wanted to hurt him. He became delusional and heard voices, just as when he heard the TV whisper, "Brad, Brad." Outwardly, he smiled.

Brad was aware he heard unreal voices. It was a creepy feeling to him. Sometimes he felt like Frank and I, especially me, were plotting against him and that my religion was a way to control him. Once, he burned my Bible. When he used marijuana, his head mellowed. Cognitively, Brad knew he was sliding down the mountain and plunging into the valley, but emotionally he needed to get high.

After the intake interview, Mark, the rehab counselor at Brighton, told us that Brad needed inpatient care because of his severe street drug use and because he was a danger to society. We told Brad we would not be bringing him home.

An adult who has a mental illness must sign themselves in for treatment, unless they are brought by the police.

One of the problems of caring for an adult who has a mental illness is that they must sign themselves in for treatment, unless they are brought by the police. This was one of the times that Brad didn't comply with our wishes. He argued with us, saying the medications and doctors didn't work. We refused to bring Brad home with us, telling him,

"We're leaving you in a safe place with food, shelter, and treatment." The rehab counselor told us that the doors to the building were open until five o'clock and that Brad would be welcomed.

We gave Brad a hug and twenty dollars, and then we left. Inside our car, we sat in the parking lot, sorting out the reasons why we abandoned our son. We knew this was in everybody's best interest. We were immobile for awhile, when I noticed snowflakes falling on the windshield. Unbeknownst to us, Brad had exited the building soon after we left him.

A miracle happened that day. Suddenly the air chilled, and the temperature dropped fifteen degrees. I knew Brad had no jacket. I knew he hated the cold, so I felt he would likely stay in the building. After we'd pulled out of the lot, we saw our son as he walked across the freeway overpass. His head was down, with his shoulders hunched to keep warm. A sudden snowstorm had appeared—a blizzard that even the Michigan weathermen hadn't predicted. Eight inches of snow fell that night. We drove home slowly, confident that our son would head back toward the shelter of rehab.

Brad did turn around. He knocked on the door, and they let him in. He told them he would stay there for the night. Mark called us. We knew Brad was safe.

Once again, he settled into the rehab routine. Once again, he was wrapped in the twelve-step promises and again, he was determined never to use pot. He learned to live one day at a time again. He tried not to worry about tomorrow while in the now.

While Brad was in rehab, Frank and I investigated our options for our son's future, where to go next, how to prevent more breakdowns, how to help, how to let go, and what medications he needed. The rehab people labeled us codependent and enablers.

The philosophies of substance abuse counselors differ from that of mental health workers; thus their treatment methods differ. This makes sense in that addiction and mental illness are separate disorders. Although all parties agree the use of street drugs is unhealthy, I found some of the differences to be in opposition to each other. After

The philosophies of substance abuse counselors differ from that of mental health workers, thus their treatment methods differ.

Brad was diagnosed with mental illness, I found some of the rehab advice did not apply when there is a mental disease. I even found some aspects of their philosophical approach harmful to the mentally ill. For example, rehab staff typically discourages all pharmaceuticals. I understand this, but this approach blinds them to the fact that people with mental illness exhibit behaviors as a result of their brain disorder. Thus a mentally ill person's life may not fall in order once they become sober. Prescribed chemical intervention is necessary to balance the disorder in the mentally ill brain.

Another difference I noted is the advice family members are given. In rehab, we were taught the vices of enabling and codependency. Again, this makes sense if the only issue is substance abuse. To avoid being an enabler, the parent must learn not to make excuses for the child's behaviors. With mental illness, however, support is necessary. Enabling and codependency are irrelevant terms.

Our son was not given the medical support he needed at any of the dual diagnosis centers where he was a patient. His disordered brain was expected to manage his own medications. The staff treated the substance abuse diagnosis but only gave lip service to the treatment for the mental illness diagnosis. At that time, there were few locations that even recognized the possibility of mental illness and substance abuse cohabitating in the same person. Our choices were limited. Where could Brad go next?

We gave Brad three options. We found three locations that offered dual diagnosis treatment.

In reality, dual diagnosis services meant the facility treated substance abuse and they were willing to store the patient's medications, if the patient supplied them. Nurses kept the medications and dispensed them, but only if the patient asked for them. We assumed the medical staff gave our mentally unstable son the medications pre-scribed by his doctor. Who expects a mentally unbalanced mind to monitor their own medications? A patient with acute mental illness is foggy, manic, depressed, angry, confused, hearing voices, or resentful. And yet, the patient was supposed to be responsible for asking for their medications.

At home, Brad complied with his medications when I handed them to him. Some were taken once a day, some twice, and some as needed. When he was at a rehab facility, I made sure his medications were at the nursing station. We also made sure the medical chart stated that he was to be called to get them. That just didn't happen. His records show he took his medications sporadically, when he remembered.

Brad chose a center in Florida. He loved the sun and the ocean. Later he told me he almost died in the ocean in West Palm. He said a voice had lured him into the ocean: "Come on in, Brad. Swim with the fish. Explore. Peace is here."

He and a buddy from the rehab center went to the beach and stayed until well past sunset. Brad was in the water most of that time. When darkness came, he saw headlights pulsing and eventually swam to shore. Meanwhile, his buddy was frantic and said, "What in the hell were you doing out there so far? I couldn't see you. You could have drowned. That undertow is strong. We are so far past curfew. We gotta get back."

When they returned to the center, Brad refused to go inside. He stayed outside and practiced basketball shots. The center called us that night, and we learned he wasn't taking his medications routinely. They wanted him to go to the local psych ward.

After that night, Brad bounced back and forth between the rehab center and the hospital's psych ward. Following his second hospital stay in Florida, it was clear to everyone that sobriety and the twelve steps toward serenity was not the path for Brad. We needed to find treatment in the mental health system.

The Florida hospital's psych facility was a good place, a few notches above our prior experiences in mental health wards. Brad moved around in attractive, sunny, locked indoor and outdoor areas. He participated in the usual group and private therapy sessions, as well as occupational therapy. In his leisure time, Brad taught himself to play piano.

We met and talked often with Brad's newest doctor, Dr. Majola, by phone and in person. Frank and I stayed in Florida for a week. This doctor listened when we told him about the medications that had been tried, which had been helpful, and which ones had been discontinued. Upon admission to the hospital, Brad presented with symptoms of "suicidal ideation with a plan, and increased delusions." Compared to other admits, he stabilized quickly. His mental alertness and his connections to reality returned within a few days. Perhaps this occurred because Dr. Majola listened to us. He immediately put Brad on mega doses of Lithium, which had successfully been tried once before.

Brad's mania quieted. He stopped pacing; he didn't have delusions of grandeur or paranoia. But he didn't care about anything either. As far as he was concerned, his life was over. He was just biding his time. He had no goals. He just went along with the program.

During the conferences in Florida, everyone agreed Brad needed to be closer to us, in some sort of a group home. Our next stop was the Holly Center in Holly, Michigan. That's where we met Dr. Tibbs, the last psychiatrist who treated Brad on this journey.

"Could she speak, my dog, I think she might ask questions which no philosopher would be able to answer. For I believe that she is (at times) tormented by the pain of existence….Small wonder if she howl at the moon that shines upon (our nighttime) world" (Lafradio Hearn, 1899. *Lunaria Lunar Journal 2009* [Friday Press, 2008]).

CHAPTER THIRTEEN

Holly

At Holly Center, Brad mourned the loss of a "normal" Brad. At the age of twenty, he was now "Brad with Bipolar." Surrounded by men and women who'd been mentally ill for years, as the youngest patient at Holly Center, he could not escape this loss. Their brains had undergone far more trauma than his. Some patients still heard voices, some were withdrawn, some paced. Most residents smoked, and all took psychotropic medications.

In classes, Brad learned about medication compliance. Unlike most young persons who need psychotropic medications, while Brad lived with us, he'd been compliant. When I gave him his medications, he took them. But the classes took compliance a step further. He learned which medications were for which symptom. He learned to become responsible for taking his own prescriptions, to monitor and become aware of his reactions to them. He became more involved in the dosage adjustments and medication changes. Within the best of his abilities, he became an educated consumer of his medications.

Dr. Tibbs, the psychiatrist at Holly Center, prescribed Clozaril for everyone I knew there. Brad was at Holly Center about a month and was depressed. He was also agitated, angry, and surly to Frank and me. He didn't want to live, and he didn't want us around. The staff and

Dr. Tibbs told us to take a break, to not see Brad for a few weeks. They advised us that he needed some space and time alone to adjust.

I remember well visiting Brad after our absence, after he'd been on Clozaril for a few weeks.

When we returned, he was outside, sitting on a step. He saw us and said, "Hi."

I asked, "How's it going?"

"Okay, I guess. They started me on the work program. I'm in maintenance. My social worker, Todd, and I built these steps."

"Do you like working in maintenance?"

"It's okay. Gives me something to do."

Although still depressed, the surliness and anger were gone. In my view, thanks to Clozaril, his personality, that gentle and pleasant soul that I'd known for eighteen years, had returned.

Gradually over the next few months, even that cheerful piece of my son returned. However, there was a price to pay. One of the side effects of Clozaril is weight gain and carbohydrate craving.

Brad had gained weight ever since Florida, where he consumed typical quantities of institutional food. I still see this today at every medical facility I've worked at. When patients are least active, huge breakfasts, lunches, and dinners are still served. Brad's body ballooned.

We were blessed when Brad was assigned to Todd, a compassionate young man, a dedicated therapist, and head of the Holly Center's maintenance program. While Brad was in maintenance rotation, they built a dock that stands there today. Residents could fish from the dock, launch a small rowboat, and jump into the lake. The four of us—Brad, me, Frank, and Todd—became friends, and we remained friends even after Todd left the center.

Rehab for the mentally ill was a new concept.

Holly Center seemed to project this attitude that it was an honor to work there. In some ways, this was true. Rehab for the mentally ill was a new concept. For mental health professionals who really cared about patients, Holly Center was revolutionary in the care, treatment, and expectations for recovery that the center provided. On the other hand, I was told by several professionals who left the facility that honor and dedication did not translate into a high salary.

While there, Brad worked in the maintenance, gardening, and kitchen rotations. After nine months, the staff proclaimed him strong enough mentally to live off campus. Everyone was pleased with his progress. He'd worked hard to adjust to his illness. Another resident, who was a few years older than Brad, was also ready to relocate. In January 1995, these two young men with mental illness embarked on their journey toward independence in the community. Russ, who coincidentally had graduated from our small-town high school, became Brad's roommate. They moved into a two-bedroom apartment in Holly.

Both remained connected to the medical support team. Several times a week, they returned to Holly Center for its Community Support Program (CSP). CSP provided scheduled consults with therapists and nurses, support groups, doctor appointments, and blood draws. We also remained involved with Holly Center. We attended family conferences as well as the summer potluck picnics and holiday parties. I initiated the family support group program. Brad became friends with other former Holly Center residents who'd graduated into the CSP program. They, too, lived on their own in apartments in Holly and in the nearby towns of Grand Blanc and Fenton. He developed friendships with former residents who lived in the same apartment complex. Whenever we visited Holly, friends often stopped in. Together, we'd found a new community—persons and families living with mental illness.

Brad's first employment after Holly Center was grounds preparation for the annual Renaissance Festival held in Holly. Next he worked in a fast food restaurant, then at an Office Depot, and later for a private company that assembled computers.

Behind the scenes, I maneuvered a different type of rebirth for my son. I phoned the pastor from the Holly Assembly of God church and referred my son to him. I told him I thought Brad would be open to an invitation to come to his church. I called because I knew how this church embraced local opportunities to spread the Word of God, and I hoped Brad would be receptive to spiritual growth. He was. He told me how this pastor from the Holly Assemblies Church visited him, and he said he would give their service a try. After that initial attendance, Brad attended regularly. I was thrilled he was able to participate in a church community.

My heart sang on the day Brad was baptized by immersion. Like me, he'd been baptized as an infant into Catholicism. But when I'd embraced the Assemblies Church, I found a rebirth within my soul as I went through the ritual of being dunked and I declared Jesus as my personal Savior. In July 1996, Brad became a born again Christian.

I believed Brad's entire world was born again.

That day birthed a new family for me also. We adopted a little boy from Frank's niece, Amy. Having been given the gift of Scott, now a toddler of twenty months, I felt complete. I once again had a young child to care for and Brad to guide and grow with. I believed Brad's entire world was born again. He had a spiritual family that we connected with, he had a peer community in Holly, he was working, and he had medical support. I had a little brother for him. Frank and I had the financial, mental, and emotional means to support him. We loved him so much. I felt the hope of renewal in his life that day.

Every month Brad made progress. In the winter of 1996, he began classes at the University of Michigan's Flint campus. I was afraid for him, fearful that he might be taking on too much. I voted for him to ease back into academics slowly, to begin at a community college and transfer to the University of Michigan-Flint later. At a family conference, which included Todd, Frank, Scott, and me, Brad was firm in his decision to resume his college studies at U of M-Flint. I wanted to go with him to enroll so that he could tap into the Americans with Disabilities Act (ADA), but he was adamant he would do this on his own. All I could do was tell him that I was available, as we all were, to support him as he pursued his bachelor's degree.

Brad sailed through U. of M.-Flint. He took a full load every semester. He joined the Computer Club and made friends in the Gaming Society. He switched his major from computer science to communications and minored in computer science. Brad liked many things and had divergent interests. He joined the *U. of M.-Flint Times* and covered sporting events for the paper.

His athletic skills converted into enthusiasm for teams and players. He became an observer in lieu of a participant. Clozaril slowed his reaction time and the weight gain disabled his mobility. One summer, he played on a community baseball league, injured his ankle, and wound up on crutches. After that, he refereed one semester but didn't like the pressure. He then became a student of sports. He became a walking statistician of the current and potential players of his favorite teams.

In the winter of 1997, he began an internship at Parkedale Pharmaceuticals. He worked at the help desk as the on-call computer expert. Again, he made new friends. Brad was a dedicated worker. When it came to working with computers, he was so focused on completing the task that he forgot about time. Often, he left late and consequently even became friendly with the evening maintenance crew.

In 1997, he received the Flint Scholar Award from U. of M.-Flint. That same year, Sam married. He first participated in a simple ceremony in our home on March 23 and then again at a big wedding with friends and family in August. Brad was the best man on both occasions. We encouraged Brad to move into his own apartment when he became a college student. We told him he could study better without a roommate. When Brad lived by himself, he discovered he liked it. He spread out his guitars and bought a cockatiel he named Paco. Besides, he wasn't really by himself. Whenever we came, his space bustled with friends. People liked him. He was a friendly, thoughtful, giving person and fun to be with. For many years, he made friends through AA and was asked to give open talks at AA meetings. He was clean and sober. He was stable on medications, and connected socially and medically to the Holly Center community.

In spring of 1999 he met a girl who would become his betrothed, Ann. Ann blended into our home and helped me fill in the gaps that came and went within my own family. After working in Detroit awhile, Sam found employment in California. Still later, he and his wife moved to Florida. Although I had a daughter-in-law, I shared more time with Ann.

Meanwhile, Frank and I found a house for Brad. He seemed content with apartment living, but when Ann lost her roommate and moved in with Brad, they were cramped. As Brad got closer to finishing his degree, it was obvious his new life would unfold in Holly. We put a down payment on a three-bedroom ranch on a tree-lined street with sidewalks. The home sat in a quiet neighborhood with a path to a nearby lake. It was newly renovated when Brad graduated from U. of M.-Flint, where he finished his degree with a grade point average of 3.3.

No sooner had Brad graduated than he accepted a computer job. Frank and I thought he was a bit impulsive. We suggested he look around more, not just take the first opportunity.

I felt Brad was worth so much more than ten dollars an hour and that his skills and good nature would be taken advantage of at that job. While I understood his excitement and desire to become independent, I wanted him to have a job closer to home with better pay. The drive from Holly to Bay City was over an hour, and the job site was in the employer's home. Brad put in tons of overtime and whenever we saw him, he talked about how unrealistic and impulsive his employer was, and how he placed unreasonable demands on the employees. I missed seeing Brad on a weekly basis. When I did see him, he'd gained more weight from eating late-night hamburgers, fries, and junk food.

Frank insisted that Brad have health coverage, given his medical condition. Brad was twenty-six when he graduated from U. of M.-Flint, and Frank had carried him all those years on his Blue Cross. When Brad took the job in Bay City, Frank continued to provide health insurance coverage for him by setting Brad up as a part-time employee in the law office. Since Brad was always updating Frank's computer systems anyway, this made sense.

When Ann and Brad announced their plan to get married, I regret to say Frank and I were not overjoyed. All parents want the best for their children. We liked Ann and supported their relationship, but marriage was another story. Seven years older than Brad, Ann was also mentally ill. We were concerned she'd hold Brad back in his progress. Both of them took prescribed medications. While pharmaceuticals may be successful in clouding the manic electricity of paranoia and the plunges of despair, they also cloud sharp thinking and mental acuity. Brad and Ann struggled daily to balance body, mind, soul, and self-esteem.

When they indicated they wanted children, I felt Brad would be a good parent, but they were at high risk to have a mentally ill child. Given Ann's functional skills, I was not confident in her parenting potential. But they loved each other, they shared intimately, and they honored and respected each other. Ann said Brad was the best guy she'd ever met, and Brad seemed content. I knew he loved her and would cherish and honor her if they got married. Brad bought her a ring for the Christmas of 2002.

Brad worked in Bay City for over a year. He put one hundred and thirty miles per day on his car, and he was working sixty to seventy hours per week. We finally convinced him to quit. After he left the Bay City job, he worked two part-time jobs—one in Frank's law office and the other at the Salvation Army's drop-in center in Holly. He looked for other jobs that would pay more and be fulfilling but felt his computer skills were already outdated. He asked me to help him with his resume as he had an interview for a part-time position at a different Salvation Army site.

We fine-tuned his resume over the phone. I helped him prepare a focus statement, and we deleted and added some of his work experience. When I asked him what he was going to wear to the interview, he said he and Ann had purchased a sport-jacket with honey-hued tweeds that flattered his ruddy skin and long torso. Ann picked out a yellow shirt and tie to complement his soft brown eyes. When he came to the law office after the interview, everyone complimented him on how good he looked. It was quite a change from his usual attire of shirts and khakis.

I didn't see how sharp my son looked in these clothes when he was alive, but I know all the details; I chose this outfit for him to wear in the coffin. My joys and anticipations of the new family that emerged when Brad's little brother was adopted had been short-lived.

CHAPTER FOURTEEN

Scott's Arrival

S cott is our adopted son, Frank's niece's child. She is the same niece, Amy, who stayed with us the summer of '91. Amy and Scott's birth father were not married when he was born, and they were lousy parents. Scott's grandparents, who live in Pennsylvania, are Frank's brother and sister-in-law. Daily, they observed how Scott and his brother, Ray, were being neglected. Scott's grandmother had her reasons for not wanting to raise him herself, so she asked me to take him. Once I took Scott in, he became an out-of-sight, out-of-mind child for them. Then, after Brad died, and I was shunned by my birth family, Scott stopped receiving any gifts and cards from my family also.

I've often wanted to ask all of them, "What did Scott do? What did he do that was so awful? How can you disengage yourselves from an innocent child?"

How can you disengage yourselves from an innocent child?

Scott arrived in our home on a Friday in July 1995. He was eight and a half months old, and his grandmother, Jane, delivered him. Amy didn't come.

A week after our infant arrived, we celebrated Frank's forty-eighth birthday. Three weeks later, I turned forty-six.

97

I knew Scott had neurological problems. I held him when he was six weeks old. Still a practicing pediatric therapist, I observed this infant's abnormal behaviors that day. He had tremors on his right side. He wasn't able to bring his hands to midline. His left and right arm movements were asymmetrical. I expressed my concerns to his birth parents, as well as to the grandparents. I was told that the doctors said Scott would be fine, that he would outgrow these problems. He'd been evaluated by specialists in Pittsburgh, and they couldn't find anything wrong. Neither mother nor child showed any elevated toxin levels in their blood. Nevertheless, I showed Amy and the birth father some handling techniques and some mini exercises that would help normalize Scott's development. I didn't expect any follow-through, but I showed them anyway.

The following June, when Jane asked me to become Scott's guardian, I felt I'd been designated by God to have this child. I felt honored. Psychologically, I prepared myself for being a mom again. My excitement grew, like a gift was coming. I dreamed of a more connected family, of the richness a little brother would bring to Brad's life, how the Pennsylvania family bonds would grow stronger and build as this new life developed in Michigan. None of that happened.

Out of all the relationship building I hoped would come with Scott's arrival, the piece that did develop was an expanded connection with Brad. I was determined to be a good mother to all three of my sons. I believed Scott would enrich our lives. Indeed, for four years or so, before Brad met Ann and while Sam was out of town, the four of us—Frank and me, little Scott and big Brad—were a cozy family. Not a typical family unit, but a family that spent time together and did lots of things with each other. We helped each other; we visited back and forth at least weekly. We ate together, celebrated special occasions, and, my favorite, we took vacations together.

When Scott first came to our home, Frank and I still attended weekly meetings with either the doctor, the case manager, or the nurse at Holly Center to discuss how Brad was responding to the medication, his participation level, and his progress within the program. We traveled to Holly each week with baby Scott in tow.

Sometimes I planned special outings for the four of us, like to the Renaissance Festival and the Huckleberry Railroad in Crossroads Village in Flint. A few times, Brad brought a girlfriend on these jaunts. This tickled me. I'd be all smiles. We all smiled. I know this because I began to take photos again. Scott's striking facial features and Brad's delight as he holds his little brother show up in every one.

Our new family unit took our first vacation together when Scott was one year old. We went to San Clemente, California, at Christmas time. It was a magical time

I began to take photos again.

for us as we walked side by side, pushing a stroller along piers that spanned over the ocean. We'd stop and watch the fishermen during the day and sit on the beach at night to watch the sunset. I felt as if I'd been asked by the heavens to mother two very special children. I felt they were safe in our care. Brad was stable, and it was so comfortable having him near us. We loved him so much.

Scott was thriving, too. I'd normalized his movements, and he was catching up developmentally and on the growth charts. With Scott

All of us in 1999.

always around, Frank and I had this healthy distraction, making it impossible for us to be "codependent" on Brad's illness. Scott was also a healthy distraction for Brad. He played with him and fed him, picked him up and carried him. They bonded. I did my best to apply the tools for effective parenting that I'd learned from my patients' families. As I raised Sam and Brad, I referenced the Dr. Spock book on child care my mother had given me when Sam was born. This time around, I was more confident and relied on my own experiences and observations.

Some of my favorite family times took place during our cleaning jaunts in Brad's apartment. For a couple years, the three of us traveled to Holly on weekends to help Brad furnish, decorate, and clean. Brad was not the neatest person in town, so I'd give everyone an assignment—run the vacuum, change the sheets, clean out the fridge, do the laundry. After Brad moved into his own place, he had Paco, that big white cockatiel. When we came, he'd let Paco out of the cage so Scott could pet him. Scott's first job was to keep an eye on Paco.

During those cleaning years, Scott grew into a preschooler and he'd find all Brad's change on the floors. That became Scott's other job—to pick up all the coins. "Brad," he'd ask, "can I keep all the coins I find on the floor?"

"Yeah, sure, Scott."

He was thrilled when one time he found seven dollars in change.

The last vacation we took together, Scott was four years old. We went to Thailand. I insisted we go there as my daughter-in-law's entire family lived there and we had never met any of them. It was two years after their marriage, the spring of 1999. Besides bonding with my daughter-in-law's family, that trip was a unique family adventure and provided us many extraordinary memories of time shared with each other.

Besides Thailand, I have traveled to other corners of the earth. I visited Africa when Sam worked there. I went to Russia on a mission trip with the church. I've cruised in Alaska and sunned in Hawaii. After my son died, I sojourned beyond the physical curves of the earth.

GENTLE POINTS

- Times shared together are the sustenance of life.
- The memories embedded forever in our souls are built from physical moments.

CHAPTER FIFTEEN

Normal vs. Paranormal

Through all my spiritual searches, I participated in many religious communities, and I felt comfortable in each and every one of them. After the death of my son, I investigated options beyond traditional religions.

My first psychic medium reading took place at a Psychic Fair in August 2003. I sat down with a woman named Kate who exuded a homespun feeling with her Irish cropped black hair, pale skin, and blue eyes.

"Today marks the fifth-month anniversary of my son's death," I said.

"Was he killed in an automobile crash? I feel an impact in front of my head and from behind," Kate said.

"No, it wasn't an auto accident, but there was an impact," I choked back my tears. "Who was there to greet my son when he crossed over? Did he have any difficulties?"

"Your son immediately went for the Light. He tells me that he knew you and his dad really loved him, but he had never felt anything like this love before. He tells me the Light was brilliant and he felt incredibly special. Your son tells me he was ready to cross over. He is happy and enjoys his work. His job on the other side is to help young people cross over who are not ready."

I felt tremendous joy hearing about Brad's life after death.

"Does your son have a little brother?"

"Yes," I replied.

"He tells me that he's watching over his little brother all the time."

"That's good. His little brother needs a lot of watching over."

Following that first psychic reading, I gradually withdrew from traditional church attendance. A year later, I received a phone call from the Methodist church.

"Pat, we've finally found someone who will be your Stephen Minister. I know you submitted your request a long time ago, but sometimes it takes awhile to find the right person. We give prayerful consideration to each request. If you're still interested, Jan will call you."

Stephen Ministers are lay caregivers.

Stephen Ministers are lay caregivers. They are regular church members with varied backgrounds who receive special training for one year in their local churches. The curriculum provides instruction in how to give one-to-one Christian care to hurting people in and around the congregation. Given our separatist society and our incompassionate culture, Stephen Ministry training is a good thing. Christian laypersons learn how to befriend the bereaved, hospitalized, terminally ill, separated, divorced, unemployed, and others who face a crisis or life challenge.

Experiencing Jan's presence whenever we got together was a great comfort for me. Jan knew how to give compassionate energy. She was a consistent beacon of love, respect, and acceptance to me. She never admonished me by saying, "Time to move on." Instead, she told me, "Your grief journey takes as long as it takes." She never treated me like a victim by lamenting, "Oh you, poor thing." Rather, Jan listened. She validated the difficulty of my journey. She said, "I can't imagine your pain," and then held my hand and allowed me to cry.

Our second meeting was in a park. Jan asked me to bring the album of Brad that I'd collated. My heart swelled and my tears fell while we sat together at a picnic table. Finally, I was able to share the beauty of my son's life with another. Finally, someone asked and was interested in connecting to my son.

I have experienced a great variety of religions. I enjoyed each denomination I joined. My church experiences are my spiritual history. My church backgrounds helped me discover who I am at my core. This knowledge is written in my mental, emotional, physical, and spiritual energies.

My new spirituality is a feeling of being connected, every day. No singular denomination can teach me all there is to know about our Creator. No single building contains exclusive rights to God. My prayer energy is different now. In silence, I talk to Brad, to the Archangels, and to the matriarchs who have preceded me in death. I'll talk to anyone who is available to listen when I need help and guidance. Sometimes I even remember to say thanks. Sometimes I just listen.

My new spirituality is a feeling of being connected, every day.

I have learned to be quiet with my thoughts. In the quiet, I am present with my soul, present with a knowing that I and my son are part of a divine universe. My new church is one of solitude, a place where I no longer stand in judgment of my own actions, trying to determine if I'm right or wrong. Rather, stillness allows the energy of the universe to transmit into my soul. When I listen to the voice of my stillness, I learn where and how to take my next steps.

"Be still and know that I am God" (Psalm 46:10, NIV).

Chapter Sixteen

Moving in Isolation

After Brad's death, it is ironic that I discovered the peace of solitude at yet another address, our fourth family home in the same hometown. We moved again because I wanted to live near people, in a subdivision. I wanted Scott to grow up in a cozy neighborhood with lots of friends around. The prior home, which we had built, was on an unpaved street without sidewalks. The driveway was two hundred yards long, remote from the street. Whenever Scott was outside, I was on alert within our 2.2-acre yard. Our dog, Silk, was his only companion. If they went down the driveway, I had to get binoculars out to see them.

Frank loved that spacious home that sprawled out among the three of us. Conversely, I felt we were conspicuous consumers. The home was so big and so remote, I felt lost and isolated. Once Scott came, I disliked having him in an upstairs bedroom with our master bedroom being downstairs. There was too much space between parent and child, and between our house and playmates. Frank, however, liked the privacy.

After I took a Feng Shui course at the local community college, my discomfort with that home was validated. When I studied the bagua map of our home and our property lines, I saw that both were shaped like a hatchet. The ideal bagua map is a nice square with nine equal sections that reflect harmony and balance. The bagua map of that house had certain sections chopped out. It looked like we designed our living spaces with the intention of cutting ourselves off from the rest of the world. I convinced Frank we needed to find a cozy neighborhood.

For this fourth house, we picked a lot on a lake. The back of our house faced west, allowing us to watch the sunsets on the water. Our new home would be smaller, our lot would be a regular subdivision size, and all the bedrooms would be upstairs.

One day in April 2003, I sat in the rocker of my new kitchen wearing purple sunglasses to shield my swollen eyes. I rocked and stared at the lake with Silk by my side. I felt suspended in a time warp, with nowhere to go and where I'd been meant nothing. I was in deep grief. It had been less than a month since Brad's death.

Outside, our yard looked like the abandoned gravel pit it was, with dirt and rocks and goose poop, and a tattered black plastic barrier at shore's edge. Scott had just come home from school and asked if he could go down by the water and play with his giant water gun. I said, "Sure. Take Silk with you."

Scott liked to throw rocks in the water and at the geese. Typical boy, he said it was fun to scare the geese and watch them flap their wings and honk. He took his gun to fire at the geese. In a conscious stupor, I stared at the scene below and saw a swan heading from the island straight toward Scott and Silk.

I stepped outside onto the deck and yelled, "Scott, put your gun down. Don't shoot at the swan."

"I'm not. I'm shooting at the geese."

"Scott, put your gun down. Look, a swan is coming toward you. He's moving really fast."

Silk and Scott turned to see the swan, who stopped and stared at Scott. With his elongated neck, the swan stood almost as tall as Scott, taller than Silk. He was so close; Scott could have touched his beak.

"Scott, just watch the swan. I've never seen a swan come so close to people before."

Some boulders that Brad had brought from the other house were piled on the shore behind Scott. Silk did not bark or move. She and the swan seemed to have this seamless stillness between them. Casually, the swan picked up a piece of wood, then put it down and then posed in silence again.

"Scott, don't move. I want to take your picture."

After I took the picture, our swan swam away.

The largest and most powerful of all waterfowl, swans can be aggressive. When they are protecting their territory from strangers, they will bite. It has been reported that once a swan broke a man's arm with its flapping wings. Yet, people all over the world consider swans to be special. Celtics associate swans with music and love. Druids believed they represent the soul and help with spiritual evolution. In Navajo tradition, the Great Spirit uses swans to work its will.

I believe the swan who visited that day was sent by Brad. I think about *The Ugly Duckling* story when I tell my swan tale. Like the ugly duckling, Brad was blind to his true being and his inner beauty while he was alive. Scott and I were given an assurance from Brad that day. He had transformed into the beauty of his spirit life, that beautiful soul part of all of us that never dies. He now lives in a universe where only the highest vibrations exist, where he knows my love, where there is no grief, where forgiveness flows like water through the channels of our hearts.

I believe Brad had transformed into the beauty of his spirit life.

Forgiveness energy came early into my spirit. Within a month after he died, I sent Brad an email asking his forgiveness. My gut knew that I must do this. I could not continue to write and talk to Brad about my love for him and my soul's yearning for his presence unless I removed some barriers between us. The barriers were things I'd said and done that hurt him.

Part of grieving is blame and doubt.

Part of grieving is blame and doubt.

In my grief, I blamed myself for so many things. My underlying stream of unconsciousness convicted me of the crimes of moving away from Cleveland and of having moved my family so many times.

I believed I was a bad girl because I was the one who moved away from my birth family. Thus I reasoned I should not expect my family to be there for me. I thought about my friends who never moved and people who die in the same homes they raised their children in. I'd always envied them and never could figure out what was wrong with me. Daily I stumbled through these abysses of grief until I finally understood what was wrong with me, why I moved so much.

It was at the summer of 2006 The Compassionate Friends (TCF) national conference where I learned to forgive myself for being me, to accept myself, and to not feel guilty. Although I had already written Brad and asked for his forgiveness, what I really needed was to forgive myself for being me.

With forgiveness as our intent, we are able to push through barriers that keep us from receiving those higher energies of love and compassion.

Forgiveness and compassion are energies that vibrate at a high level, unlike the more dense energies of guilt and resentment, and bitterness and jealousy. With forgiveness as our intent, we are able to push through barriers that keep us from receiving those higher energies of love and compassion. Just as I needed forgiveness from my son in order to feel his love and be able to send mine, so too have I forgiven my parents, my spouse, my in-laws, friends, pastors, and anyone and everyone who may or may not be aware of my pain. That is how I learn to hold no one responsible for my pain other than myself. I believe that I hold the key to my own joy. It's up to me whether I let love in or whether I block it with guilt and anger. Day by day, I honor my pain and my joy. Each day I choose which lessons to learn. I have struggled with the lesson of love

I believe that I hold the key to my own joy.

from Scott's parents, who neglected him. With difficulty, I claim the gift of life they gave him and the love in their hearts that gave him to me. With delight, I claim the lesson from Silk's near death experience.

On January 29, 2004, Silk was thirteen years old and arthritic. It was winter and my backyard lake was brushed with fresh snow. Two swans hovered near the island's edge, and a flock of geese sat on the icy water.

That afternoon, Scott and his friend broke winter's stillness by whacking the ice with hockey sticks. I viewed them from the great room windows while I removed Christmas tree trims, my collection of mementos from the past.

When my daughter-in-law arrived to help, I asked her to put Silk outside with the boys. Although mentally alert, Silk was physically challenged. Over the summer, she'd injured her knee and walked on three legs. She continued to climb the stairs with difficulty and walked with a slight limp.

I glanced out the window. My mind registered and processed: *There are tracks in the snow on the lake. They weren't there a minute ago.*

Then, I realized they were Silk's paw prints. Her steps carved a path from our shore toward the geese. The path ended at a hole with Silk's head inside. She was at least thirty feet from shore's edge and had fallen through the ice.

I donned my coat and boots and went to the garage for something to rescue my dog, who was treading water in the middle of a frozen lake. I grabbed Scott's circle swing with a twelve foot rope attached.

I ran to the lake and walked on the fragile ice toward her, but my steps sank to the bottom. I could not possibly rescue her.

When my eyes met Silk's from across the lake, I knew the only thing I could give her was my voice. I encouraged her, "Good girl, Silk. It's okay. Good girl. Mommy's coming."

She responded. Every time I spoke to her, she'd reach on top of the ice with her paws to pull herself up, but every time the ice cracked and she slipped under. I believed it was the last day I would ever see her.

Meanwhile, my daughter-in-law ran next door and asked some moving men for help. They came, but as they walked into the ice, they also sank. Then one of the movers decided to jump into the neighbor's boat. We all pushed the boat through the ice and water, making it about halfway to Silk. The mover inside the boat paddled the rest of the way to my trapped dog. He reached for her paws and pulled her up. She looked like a straight arrow coming out of that hole.

She'd been treading water for about forty-five minutes at the time of rescue. The rescuer brought her to me. When I petted her, she felt like an icicle. Given her disabilities, I was not very hopeful about her recovery.

My daughter-in-law scooted Silk to the walk-out basement where she had a space heater and blankets ready.

What happened next is unbelievable. About twenty minutes after resting in the basement, Silk tried to come up the stairs. I heard my daughter-in-law command, "No, Silk. Stay." Silk heard me come in. She wanted no part of waiting and warming up alone. Up the stairs, she bounced. She scrambled up those steps faster than she ever had.

An alert and wet Silk barked and shook water all over the great room. Then she plopped down on her rug near the kitchen, licked her coat, and looked around, pleased.

That night I decided to attend the monthly Compassionate Friends meeting. Compassionate Friends is an international self-help organization for bereaved parents. While driving to the meeting, I thought, *Brad must have had something to do with keeping Silk alive. Is it possible he held her up while she treaded the water? There's no way she could have survived that frigid water for that long at her age. I think I just watched a miracle. I thought for sure Silk was going to die. Then she could have joined Brad on the Other Side. But she's alive and in better shape than before she fell in. Why would Brad do that? Why would he rescue her? Why wouldn't he want her up there with him? If Heaven is such a great place and Brad is there, then he and Silk could be happy there together. I wish Brad had been rescued too.*

My Compassionate Friends at the meeting answered my questions.

"Brad knows you need Silk. He knows you need her more than he does."

"He wants her to be with you, to give you comfort."

"He knows you couldn't handle her death now."

Until the day she died, Silk's body was better when she came out of that ice than it was before she went in.

GENTLE POINTS

- Miracles are, have been, and always will be a part of life.

- When our hearts are open to all possibilities, the events that defy the physical laws of nature can flow toward us.

- When a bereaved parent is gifted by miraculous signs from beyond, our joy is unsurpassed and will not be stifled by scientific rationalizations.

Chapter Seventeen

A Healing Conference

I never attended the monthly meetings of The Compassionate Friends (TCF) with the same regularity and enthusiasm I did when I joined other groups, like Church and Society. I went to TCF more on an as-needed basis. As June 2006 approached, I attended more as the focus of the meetings changed. The annual national conference was to be held in Dearborn, a city about a thirty-minute drive from my home. With Michigan as the host state, all the local chapters stepped forward and volunteered to decorate tables, organize speakers, and sponsor activities. It's a huge event that requires a tremendous amount of work. As the call for volunteers went out, our small family of Frank, Scott, and I helped a little. The miniature tissues in the conference goodie bags were donated in memory of Brad that year. On a Saturday before the conference, Scott helped the committee pack the goodie bags, as he skated from bag to bag with his roller shoes.

The members of my chapter were so enthusiastic about prior conferences they'd been to that I felt I should go since it was so close to home. By this time, I'd reached a sort of insulated state of equilibrium with my grief. The prolonged sobbing that left me exhausted in those early months had tapered off to periodic cleansing cries. I had a weekend physical therapy job and had begun to treat myself to things like anti-aging facials and cellulite reducing procedures. I enrolled in a tap dancing class and had performed with my class at a recital. I attended some writing workshops. I minimized communication with friends and family if I felt the conversations would be toxic. I felt I was where I could be on my grief journey, that I functioned as best as I could. I was not convinced a conference that looked back at my sorrow would benefit me.

But I went anyway, and I'm glad I was wrong. The compassion at the conference was real. The energy was healing. The tenderness was so gentle, I inhaled it. The acceptance so tangible, I touched it. The presence of unconditional love was so loud, I heard it. I laughed and I cried. By Saturday afternoon, I called Frank to tell him I planned to stay for dinner, the candle-lighting ceremony, and evening classes.

Little did I know, the best was yet to come.

All I knew about the candle-lighting ceremony was that Alan Pedersen would be singing. I'd never heard of Alan. He is a bereaved father whose daughter Ashley died at age eighteen in an auto accident. Alan is easy to see because he is this huge, bear kind of a guy. At the conference, I had metal buttons made from photos of Brad, which I had pinned onto my blouse. At different times, I saw this big guy walking around who bore an uncanny resemblance to my son. They both have gentle smiles, warm eyes framed with wired glasses, dark wavy hair, broad shoulders, and round cheeks.

The compassion and tenderness present at national conferences for the bereaved can be very healing.

After dinner, the lights were dimmed and the ceremony began as the first person lit their candle. That first person then passed the flame to the person who stood next to them. In the background, I heard music, the strum of Alan's guitar. I was engulfed by the spirits around me. An ambience of hypnotic strength descended upon us while Alan sang "Tonight I Hold This Candle." Brad's energy caressed me as I swayed in the rhythm of the gentle refrain.

Tonight I hold this candle, in memory of you,
Hoping some way, somehow my love will shine through.
I close my eyes, lost in the glow.
There are so many things I want you to know.
This candle says I love you. This candle says I miss you.
This candle is saying I remember you.
When I'm holding it toward heaven, it feels like you are near.
If you're looking down tonight and see this candle burning bright,
it says I'm wishing you were here.
Someday, some way I'll see you again.
I'll hold you in my heart until then.
Alan Pedersen, www.everashleymusic.com.

The hardest part of that ceremony was to open my eyes. When a musician creates a song, when he discovers the right combination of words and sounds, we say that creation was inspired. It is a work that has evolved from a delicate balance of the Creator's physical, emotional, mental, and spiritual energies. That song then has the power to reach out and touch other souls at their deepest level. When my soul hears music that touches the chaos within me, I experience a pattern of comfort. Songs have the potential to bring harmony to the turmoil of our thoughts and feelings. I believe that Alan opens the souls of many bereaved parents and brings order to our confusion. His songs express our deepest yearning, a connection to our children. It has been said that when we laugh, our hearts open up, and when we cry, our souls open. When our souls open, healing energy can pour in.

When the lights came back on and I forced my eyes open, I saw who Alan was. I believed that Brad's energy channeled into Alan that night, and I had to have a hug. I headed straight for the stage just like that swan that swam straight from the island a few years before. I showed Alan my button of Brad.

When my soul hears music that touches the chaos within me, I experience a pattern of comfort.

"Who does this look like?" I asked.

"Me." And he gave me the most awesome hug that will forever be embedded in every cell of my body. That night I felt a moment of wholeness, as if my soul had been embraced by my son.

Alan's new career is traveling all over the country sharing his music with bereaved parent groups. He tells us, "God wrote "Tonight I Hold This Candle." I consider myself fortunate that he asked me to hold the pen."

Alan was not the first guy Brad channeled through to me, nor was his song the first gift of music from my son. By May 2003, my hair needed a cut and color. I couldn't return to my stylist from before. Sit in a beautician's chair for a few hours sharing friend and family anecdotes, two months after my son's death? No way. I had to find a new stylist. A friend suggested I try Ron. He knew nothing about me or Brad, and I planned to keep it that way. After we exchanged typical pleasantries, Ron somehow meandered his way onto the topic of his psychic abilities. He told me about events from his past that evidenced his ability to communicate with spirits. From the time he was in sixth grade, he had realized something unusual was going on in his head. He spoke of various predictions he'd made of events and people. His family freaked when he'd do this. Ron, now in his fifties, was raised in a strong Church of God home. His grandfather was a preacher. In fact, when his grandfather died, Ron was awakened that morning at 3:00 a.m. by a thunderbolt of light. Before his mom got the phone call later that morning, Ron already knew about his grandfather's death. During my hair session, Ron told me at least five times, "I don't know why I'm sharing my psychic abilities with you. Very few people know about this. I usually don't talk about it because most people freak out. My parents believed I spoke from the devil."

I said, "No, that ability is not of the devil. It's a gift from God."

As he continued to share his experiences, Ron stated, "I really want to share with you what happened when my mom died."

His mom had been diagnosed with cancer. One day while he visited her, he made a request, "Mom, after you die, would you come back and let me know somehow if everything you've taught me about life after death is true?"

Ron's mom protested, but he said, "Mom, you don't have to give me an answer now. Take your time. Pray about it. Give me an answer when you're ready."

A year later, she told Ron that she would come back and visit, as long as she wouldn't be breaking any rules.

Besides being a stylist, Ron is also a musician. About a year after his mom died, he was driving on a Saturday afternoon to a jamming party while listening to rock tunes. Suddenly, his head was filled with different music, a soft melody, not from the radio's rock station. At the same time, his mouth spit out words. While his mouth moved and spoke, music blared in his brain. He almost got into an accident, so he pulled over and wrote in shorthand the words his mouth formed. Instead of playing music with his buddies that day, he went home and wrote the words in longhand and sounded out the chords and notes of the music he'd heard.

Ron then asked me, "Who do you think bought me my first guitar? Who do you think took me to music lessons? Who do you think helped me practice?"

I said, "Your mom."

He said, "Yes, so don't you think it's logical that she would answer my request with a song?"

He told me how the hairs on his arms stood up even as he retold me his story. In the beginning, as Ron told his story, I misted up. By the time he recited the words to the song his mother gave him, that familiar gush of tears poured out. Ron ran around to find tissues and kept apologizing, "I'm so sorry; I didn't mean to upset you."

As my tears subsided, I said, "Ron, I know why you told me this story."

I told him of Brad's death, and I told him how I found the *Pieces of You* cassette tape in Brad's car and how Jewel's music soothed my soul. I'd never even heard of Jewel before I found that tape. It seemed like each tune on that album was meant for me, especially the last one,

"Angel Standing By." Ron told me that Jewel had been in Michigan for a while and that he had jammed with her.

I believe that all of these experiences have been messages from my son.

The affirmations I experienced that day continue to be with me. I do not believe that all these connecting events were random incidents. Rather, I believe these miraculous coincidences have been signs and messages sent from my son.

Here is Ron Stahl's song, "In The Last Days of My Life."

In the last days of my life, will I look back in strife?
Search for what I've been or have I cheated myself again?
In the last days of my life, when I think of all of you,
Wish you love and happiness and may your minds be laid to rest.
In the last days of your lives, we smile and pay the price.
Can you say you gave it your best or did you just lay down and waste a life?
In the last days of your lives, have you left some things undone?
I have strived to better this world. How about you?
In the last days of our lives, it all comes down to Christ.
Give your love and soul to heaven. Lay down and die in peace.

CHAPTER EIGHTEEN

I Had a Dream

I was just coming awake. Lo and behold, you were lying right next to me. I rolled over and kissed you on the cheek. Then I figured, I'd better hurry up and hug you before you disappear. So, I gave you a big hug, so incredibly happy to have you there and to be able to wrap my arms around you for a bear hug once again. And then I knew I had another minute, so I asked you if it was true: Were you really happier now, in heaven, than on earth? And you smiled and nodded your head yes.

My first visitation dream. The sensation of hugging Brad that morning will forever remain with me. The intensity of the experience is what distinguishes a visitation dream from other dreams. In dream books, dreams are categorized and labeled, but the dream that really matters to the bereaved is the visitation dream, dreams that affirm that our beloved is okay. But there are reasons for everyone, and especially for the bereaved, to pay attention to the messages our dreams tell us. Dreams are the way our subconscious manages our physical, emotional, spiritual, and mental energies. In sleep, we connect with another world. In that space, our soul brings us images and symbols designed to give us insight and healing.

Visitation dreams are affirmations that our beloved are alive in spirit.

Dream study is a part of what I do now. After my dream visit from Brad, I yearned for more. My motivation to enter this study was to see and understand any and all images of my son. But I was a little afraid because not all dreams are pretty. My studies have paid off in healing connections. As I searched for messages from my son, I discovered myself. In the space of universal love, there is no death. I believe my son's passing was not of my design but of another. Through dream analysis, I have seen how my son and I are entwined forever, how his passing is a part of life's cycle. We live, we breathe, we die, and we begin anew.

I now see how my son and I are entwined forever, how his passing is a part of life's cycle.

Like most people, before I embarked on this dream journey, I rarely remembered any of my dreams. As I developed the skill to remember and record my dreams, I was able to fill journals with my nighttime visions. But I was clueless as to their meaning. All this great stuff being spoken to me and it was in a foreign language. I sought out a dream analyst.

I have never been the same since. My first dream analysis was worth a thousand counseling sessions. That interpretation gave me a glimpse of the real me. And I liked what I saw. This surprised me. I thought there was a hidden me that was seriously ugly. Instead, the disapproving messages I believed about myself began to wash away as I learned more about me through my dreams. I felt my guilt dissolve. The dream I had analyzed was about my inner child. I'd chosen that particular dream for analysis because it included Brad. The analyst told me I picked it because my spirit knew the messages I needed to hear.

In my dream, Brad sat in a pickup truck. He rolled down his window as I walked by on a sidewalk. As I walked, I held the hand of a little girl who had a limp. Brad told me that a friend had called him and told him the plumbing in the Holly house was broken. I smiled at my son and said, "Well, we'll just have to fix it."

In the analysis, Brad represented the gentle part of my personality and in dream language, water symbolizes emotions and the plumbing represented the pipes through which my emotion flowed. She said my unconscious knew that my fundamental connections, the emotional network of my life, had fallen apart. My reply showed that I was confident I would mend. That dream revealed huge chunks of my iceberg, pieces to my

The universe uses dreams to reveal information to us, and these messages are always delivered in love.

life's puzzle, lost parts that I'd buried. And it was all good. The universe uses dreams to reveal information to us, to impart knowledge about our lives. These messages are always delivered in love. I felt empowered and embraced. I was in awe and in peace after my dream analysis was completed.

In February 2007, I enrolled in a "Dreaming with the Archangels" class, a thirty-day journey with Michael, Raphael, Gabriel, and Uriel. Since I wanted to know more about dreams, I didn't let the title prohibit me from attending the course. I'm glad I took the journey. There is a new energy within and around me. I am surrounded by vibrations unknown to me before. I now experience a universe that is more connected than disjointed. A part of my divine purpose has become sharing my dream knowledge with bereaved parents. My new charity work is giving my workshop, "How Dreams Heal," to bereaved parent organizations.

As my Archangel class ended, the fourth anniversary of Brad's death approached. I planned to honor myself and my son with another psychic medium visit. I phoned and set up an appointment with Kate. Talking with Kate helped me connect with Brad. Through Kate, Brad encouraged me to continue writing this book. He is there, helping me write it.

I have learned that suffering can burn away the ego. From the ashes, a naked soul emerges. As Sister Lucia told me when I counseled with her, I have awakened to the truth of the inner me. She said more of me would be revealed as I emerged from my grief. My past baggage was stuffed with identities from outdated images and expectations. Every role I identified with disintegrated after Brad died. I could not be a good Christian. I could not be a dutiful daughter or the handmaiden wife. A pediatric physical therapist was what I was but could no longer be. The roles from my past surrounded my soul. Everything I'd been and done triggered pain. All associations scorched me.

My grief journey has forced me to delve deep into the core of me.

My grief journey has forced me to delve deep into the core of me when I couldn't be around my old identities. The deeper I go, the more of me I discover. Brad's death has placed me on a soul discovery journey. I do not walk alone. There are bereaved mothers who have traveled before me, some walk with me, and some lag behind.

I've changed. Each day I learn some of life's hardest lessons: how to honor the truth of me, how to forgive me, and how to be grateful for my lessons. I learn to pursue my natural instincts. By so doing, I am in sync with my Creator. By so doing, I eternalize the love between my son and myself. Through my son's death, I've learned to tap the "me" within that was hidden, the "me" that I didn't trust to let out. I feared all judgments, either from others or of my own imagining. Fear paralyzed my essence. Through me, Brad's life lives on. After one's child dies, what is left to fear? His passing has been a catalyst to my growth and enlightenment. I'd been told this and hated to hear it. But deep within me, I have found this to be true. In honor of my son, I

Our souls are linked for eternity.

gain strength. Together, he and I fulfill a purpose. Within a seamless connection, we realize our lessons. We find delight. Our souls are linked for eternity.

SOUL EVOLUTION

Birds dine on leftover crumbs offered after your meals.

   The sight of wings that flutter gives you delight.

You enjoy the sweet sparrows who feast on your fragments,

      With no songs in their throat, they express only pleasant peeps.

Once I was content. A cheerful chick who fed from those tidbits left on the ledge.

   Grief took over, forced me to plunge.

I stumbled below, through paths underground.

   I staggered above, fell into strange clouds.

Charms of old and flights of fancy burned off as I walked through the fires.

   Sorrow transformed me, freed my soul.

I learned I'm not a bird with a cheerful chirp.

   Instead I tread on Aquarius' edge.

I cavort on shores, each step a dance, each dance an explore.

   My song long hidden now is emerged.

I sing in harmony with those who are present when I appear.

~Tricia Wolfe

CHAPTER NINETEEN

Celebratory Survivor

As a caterpillar sheds its cocoon and morphs into a butterfly, the old me learned to cast off the old skins so a transformed me could emerge. Unlike the butterfly, whose metamorphosis is part of his normal life cycle, my transformation was trauma induced. My morph was more like the leaf that the caterpillar is born upon each spring. In summer, that leaf nourishes him, but in fall that leaf drops off the tree, decays, and then dies during winter. Come spring, a new leaf grows in its place nourished by a ground enriched by the fallen leaves. This cycle of birth, life, decline, and death repeats each season, every year, through many life cycles. Brad's traumatic death brought me many fall seasons when I learned to shed the useless. I experienced many winters, cycles of time when all I could do was embrace the solitude of nothing. I see spring now as I continue to learn what needs to be shed to make way for new growth. I search the grounds for places to plant my summers that blossom. The rhythm of the universe. Reflected in the four seasons. Growth follows birth. Life emerges from growth. Death follows life.

While still in the winter of my grief, a flyer showed up in my mailbox seeking to recruit physical therapists who would work part-time or weekends at an extended care facility. Working weekends with the elderly. There were probably very few physical therapists lining up for that job. They would probably hire me even though my experience in geriatrics was nonexistent and I hadn't worked in four years.

I constructed my resume, secured an interview, and convinced myself I would not cry during the interview—that I really wanted this position. I had cried at prior career guidance appointments, so I knew I was vulnerable. The trigger at the career guidance sessions was always, "Why do you want a job?" The only reply I could think of was, "My son died a year ago. I need a distraction."

During the interview for the weekend job, I did choke out some of my replies, but there were no tears. I was offered the position and returned to work as a physical therapist in August 2004.

I'm glad I followed my instincts and returned to therapy work. It was a huge decision. I expected my re-entry into therapy work to be difficult. I knew I was still fragile, that I had a grief disability, but I didn't know how my symptoms would play out and neither could anyone else. Grief symptoms are unpredictable and know no timeline or chronology. In our culture, we've lost those outward indicators that tell us when a person with grief is onboard. Remember when widows wore black for a year after their spouse died? Everyone recognized the significance of their journey and accepted the widow's condition. For a bereaved parent, there is no single word to describe us and when we mention our condition, we often feel like we have the plague. No one knows what to do or say, and no one wants to talk about the unthinkable, the death of a child.

I experienced small successes in my therapy work, and it spurred me on for the future.

After I returned to work, I often felt like I was in a state of suspension. I watched myself, waiting to see how my bereaved condition would unfold. Gradually, I learned how to be around people again. I discovered how to protect myself from and avoid triggers of pain, while at the same time focusing on providing physical therapy services to my patients. Renewal of my therapy career was not an easy path, but it was a necessary one for me. It was necessary to reclaim that lost part of my soul, that spiritual energy that enjoys helping people. In my work with the elderly, I found a way to honor and respect that part of myself. I evolved during those weekends as I emerged from

I'd found a way to honor my past and respect myself in the present.

my self-imposed shell. I gained a new physical therapist friend, one who told me how much she appreciated me.

"You have a passion for your work, a rare thing these days," she said.

Over time, I could even laugh with my fellow colleagues, as we shared the humor that emanates from common work experiences.

Besides helping me recapture my self-esteem and ability to be among the nonbereaved, my weekend job became an escape from real and perceived pressures to be a normal family. Being a Midwesterner, I was ingrained with the idea that Saturdays and Sundays are family days. Since Frank had always considered there were seven work days on the calendar, I could escape the heaviness of my own expectation of what Frank, Scott, and I should do on weekends. As my job unfolded, I realized I could flee from all holiday celebrations. I signed up to work Thanksgiving, Christmas, Easter, and Mother's Day, and was thrilled to do so, especially when the pay was time and a half. That job provided me a place of refuge for those days.

Another activity that brought me healing was writing. Writing down thoughts brought order to my chaos. My writing journey began when I emailed my thoughts to Brad a few days after his death. While I'd always been an avid reader, the

Journaling is known to be healing for the soul.

only writing I'd done in my past was in academic assignments, my teenage diaries, and some travel logs from our vacation days. The more I emailed Brad, the more I found comfort in the written word. Soon, I switched from emails to journaling in a notebook. At first, my journals were a potpourri of letters to myself, to Brad, to God, to anyone who could hear the words that I could not speak. Later, I used lyric to soften my laments and whines and cries. The discipline of writing my thoughts on paper helped me shape the jumble of energies that churned within. Writing helped me connect with my soul as I strived to find a purpose in all of this disorder.

My mission became to write a book that would honor my son.

I recorded events from my son's life and patterned them into stories. That discipline of the search for the right word, the structure of a sentence, the development of a paragraph, and the alignment of paragraphs into a whole gave me a focus and helped me find harmony. My mission became to write a book that would honor my son. I wanted to write a book that would touch others' souls and bring compassion into this hurting world. Through my son's death, my own life has evolved on a path I could not have foreseen or pursued.

Writing has played a role in the expansion of my womanhood. In my past, fears paralyzed me from being all of me. My energies were focused on being a compliant girl, a faithful wife, a dedicated mother, and a genuine therapist. I wanted to please others. On the outside, I was fine. The world viewed the image of a loyal wife inside a successful marriage, who nurtured her children and had a career. Inside, my soul suffocated as parts of me were rejected and stifled. There was a passionate, playful, flirtatious, and feminine me who lay dormant. Instead, I constantly strived to be the good girl I was expected to be. Now, I no longer strive to fit an image that others would have for me.

The world views me differently, or perhaps I should say the world sees more of me now. I no longer seek to fit into someone else's image of what I am supposed to be and do. It's just me. I take responsibility for my own messes, for my own actions, for deeds that happen to please or displease others. I make no apologies for being who I am.

In the past, I either felt I needed to apologize for not doing things the "right" way or I felt guilty when I failed to accomplish what was expected of me. I held myself captive to the image of the cultural standard of what a successful woman should look and act like. Prisoners in captivity learn how to best follow the rules. A prisoner strives to demonstrate the right behaviors in order to minimize judgments and criticisms. I was a prisoner of my own design.

When a child dies, many images die. The image of a happy family dies. The image of a successful parent dies. That is not to say that these images will be forever. It is possible to restore some of the old image and build new ones. I have shed many images. I have worked hard to shed myself of guilt. In the shedding process, I have left behind what I perceive to be outdated and toxic expectations of me. The naked me that has emerged is a woman who has joy and passion and spontaneity. I have lost so much; what else have I to lose? Nothing. I have everything to gain as I discover all of me. I have discovered that life is about lessons. I pay close attention each day to my lessons, to this fabric of life. I touch my fabric. I embrace each piece of it. I honor the design. This knowing, this discovery, that both life and death are divine gifts has brought me into my summer seasons. It is in this summer of my life where I grow and bloom.

"Hope is the thing with feathers that perches in the soul and sings the tune without words and never stops at all" (Emily Dickinson).

The feather that tickles my soul everyday is Brad. His spirit is perched deep within me. He sings a tune that compels me to celebrate life. No matter what I encounter, I know my son's voice of hope will never stop. Having lost and abandoned so much of my past, a sense from within me has been established that fills in that gap. It is a theme of life I carry with me all days. This theme is a knowing that I have nothing else to lose by being open to all of me, by being true to myself. I have a sense that the spirit of my son is perched on a branch in my soul. *"All changed, changed utterly; a terrible beauty is born"* (W.B. Yeats, *"Easter1916" and Other Poems*).

CHAPTER 20

Naked Goddess

It is still strange and not the way it is supposed to be, that I can still tap into this goddess energy that surrounds me. When I began writing this book, I was a married woman living in a spacious home on a lake in Michigan working occasionally as a physical therapist while mothering a preadolescent Scott. Now I am a divorced woman living in an apartment in a gray city in Indiana, where I teach full-time and occasionally parent my teenage son. I was a bereaved mom when I began this journey and I will always be a bereaved mom. That bereavement energy is woven into the fabric of my soul for eternity. And, as I've attempted to tell in this tale, the death of my son cleared out the worn and tattered threads of my soul, thus allowing a new pattern to emerge. It is this new pattern of me that has discovered the goddess energy. I feel the flow of the divine feminine. I am connected to the matrilineal spirit that is available to all women.

How can I be such an oxymoron? How could a religious woman, now divorced, who bore one son out of wedlock, birthed another son with mental illness who was killed, and adopted another with special needs possibly ever feel like a goddess?

I can because I have learned to honor the life endowed to me by death. I honor the womb that birthed my son. I experience the essence of life. I embrace womanhood, which inspires energy in me. I feel as if Brad opened the door to forces of life that were closed to me before. I believe that the elemental energies that come from the earth are universal gifts from our Divine Creator. Each of us has the opportunity every day to decide how we will design our lives with these.

Like a tree, we are given the earth's energy. From the ground, from earth's natural resources, our physical energy grows. My body grows in strength and sustains health as I soak in natural nourishments from this physical world. Exercise and eating vital foods are ways I sustain my physical energy. But I don't stop there. Being a woman, I love makeup and cute shoes and manicures and other physical adornments that are fun and frivolous. I also know I am blessed. The cost of a face-lift is something I could afford. Looking younger nourishes a youthful spirit in me. That fine hair I inherited from my mom is no longer a bane for me. Instead, those hairs have become anchors for the hair extensions I am also lucky enough to afford. And I intend to wear my hair extensions to my grave! The better I look, the better I feel, the more confident becomes the wiggle in my walk.

As every good Catholic woman was taught before me and after me, the primary purpose for our being is procreation. No longer bound by that image, I now acclaim this awakening of my femininity. I celebrate womanhood. I love being the half of the race that holds the womb, where life is created.

Water is another universal gift. Our mental energy is like water. Our thoughts are like a stream that flows in a pattern. By using my mental energy, I am able to establish long-term goals and realistic expectations. In my new life, I have fiscal responsibilities and reasonable expectations on how to live the rest of my life. Mental energy enables me to learn the causes and effects of my actions, how and why things happen. I learn the tough stuff from my mistakes and from others' mistakes. And I learn from the fun stuff, like ballroom dancing and online dating. I am grateful for my intellect, for my ability to teach and learn, to participate in book clubs, and to plan for my financial future.

My mental energy harnesses learning from all lessons. I strive for clarity in my thought patterns. I do not know exactly which lessons I will learn from each day or from each new relationship I encounter, but I know I am on a path that is open to all that is good, with ease and grace.

Like the warmth of the sun, we are all gifted with emotional energy. From the element of fire we receive love and passion, joy and laughter, sadness and grief. Not every day is a goddess day for me. I still feel sorrow. On those days, I allow for its presence. As I breathe, my hurts flow through me. I still my heart and inhale the message. In time, I am able to exhale my pain into the universe. Then, I am ready to sample new delights. Perhaps I'll hear a special song, or I will see a bird at my window. Sometimes I sense a message has come from Brad in the form of a new friend or in an affirmation of an action I've taken. In this discovery of my emotional energy, I have learned to love and take care of me. I know that my son lives in a place of unconditional love, a place where the universal delights of joy and love, peace and kindness reside. When I find those treasures, I wink and say, "Thanks, Brad."

Our gift of spiritual energy is like the element of air. Our spiritual energies give expansion to our physical beings. I am, and always will be, open to miracles, events in life that cannot be *Without death, we do not know how to celebrate life.* explained away by physical science. My spiritual energy gives me an awareness of my connection to others and to each moment of the day. Just as air becomes wind when there is turbulence, so has my spiritual energy supported me as I accepted a new job in a new state. In due time, tumultuous winds die down, the air again becomes still and invisible. So too has the turmoil of being single in a strange city, now that a new job has settled into my soul. Each day I breathe a quiet trust in my Divine Creator and in my son's eternal life. I have learned that what matters spiritually is the universal connection I touch with every human being, no matter their race or religion or residence. We are all joined in the breath of life.

It has been said that laughter opens the heart, tears open the soul. Grief over the loss of my son opened my life force. My feminine energy, buried for so long, has been restored. Today, and for all the days I continue to exist on this earth, I celebrate my intrinsic womanhood. I claim the history of my forbearers as my own as I move forward into a life that sustains growth.

P atricia Wolfe grew up a daughter in a suburb of Cleveland where she graduated from an all-girl Catholic high school. After receiving her degree in physical therapy from Ohio State University, she and her husband moved to a suburb of Detroit, where they raised their three sons. An avid reader and lifelong learner, Tricia went on to earn her master's degree in education from the University of Michigan. In 2003, their second son, Brad, was killed in Holly, Michigan. "My son's death launched my need to write," Tricia explains.

Recently divorced, she now lives in Indiana where she teaches physical therapy. Each day she strives to breathe a life bequeathed with celebratory energy. She hopes her work will influence men and women to reach inside their souls and embrace life's lessons, especially the lessons learned from trauma. A self-proclaimed book clubaholic, Tricia is also passionate about dating, dancing, dreaming, and travel. Please visit her website at www.patriciawolfebooks.com.

Additional Endorsments

"As a professional who has worked in the mental health field, I found Wolfe's book illustrates many aspects of a family's journey through the mental health system. Being the parent of a bipolar child is never easy. With anguish and love, Wolfe describes her feelings as she and her spouse seek care for their son. In spite of frustrations, detours, and a tragic accident, there is a sense of hope on every page. I highly recommend this book as an educational read and a comfort to anyone who has a family member with mental illness."

~Rev. Dennis M. Cissna, COTA, Captain (Chaplain Indiana Guard Reserve), Department Chair, Occupational Therapy Assistant Program, Fort Wayne, IN, Pastor, Sovereign Grace Baptist Church, Culver, IN

"*A Heart Torn, A Soul Mended* describes the life of a mother whose son suffered with mental illness prior to his death. The author's story is both tragic and inspirational as she struggles to cope with her son's death while overcoming society's expectations of the perfect wife, mother, and bereaved parent. Bereaved parents everywhere will find that this book adds meaning and understanding to their grief journey."

~Chris and Stella Otterstedt, co-leaders of The Compassionate Friends, Fort Wayne, IN Chapter

"Tricia Wolfe's story is one of how rebirth and renewal can emerge out of extreme grief. It is a journey of courage and inner strength, of searching and willingness to see—and more importantly to feel. Few would choose this journey, but those who take it emerge stronger and more aware. And once begun, it is a journey that never ends. Those who read this story can be grateful to the author for her willingness to share not only her story but also her inner secret heart and the growth that comes from embracing life's lessons."

~Pamela Burke, Stephen Minister

"*A Heart Torn, A Soul Mended* is an insightful and powerful piece of work that provides enlightenment into an area of victimology that is seldom addressed—victims who are survivors of excessive and unnecessary police force. In this candid, thoughtful, and revealing book, Wolfe captures her innermost thoughts and feelings through a focused and simplistic prose that leaves you gasping to know more about her pain and transformations that have occurred as a result of the gifts left behind by her son Brad. Her experience clearly demonstrates the brutality of a stoic criminal justice system that victimizes survivors of lost loved ones at the hands of ill-equipped police. *A Heart Torn, A Soul Mended* is a must read and an excellent supplemental reader for any victimology course because it provides substantial insight into the pain and anguish of those tossed aside by the system that is intended 'to protect and to serve.' Wolfe should be applauded for courageously sharing her most difficult and intimate journey with us. Having taught criminal justice courses for more than twenty years, I highly recommend *A Heart Torn, A Soul Mended*."

~Daniel Gutierrez, Professor of Criminal Justice